Captain of
My Own Ship

SUNSHINE'S STORY

By

Jennifer Dowker

Captain of My Own Ship
Sunshine's Story
By Jenifer Dowker

FORWORD

You know how most fictional novels say "This book is a work of fiction. Any references to historical events, real people, or real places are used fictitiously. Other names, characters, places, and events are products of the author's imagination, and any resemblance to actual events or places or persons living or dead is entirely coincidental."?

I wish, with all my heart, that this statement was truth in my book, in my story. The fact is, that it is real. (I wonder how many of the rest are too). This fact makes it more compelling, more obvious that anyone can walk through the darkest moments of life and overcome monumental obstacles to rise shining and full of love for this life.

Some of the names have been changed to protect those involved. There was no ill-intent in the creation of this book, for any involved in the 'Sunshine Story.' There is no one demon that can be blamed for anyone's troubles. Alcoholism, abuse, death, and so many more issues can weigh a person down or can be the catalyst for their rising. This is a story of rising.

The purpose of this book is threefold:

1. To show you, the reader, steps to follow to help you achieve your own dream and help you to barrel through your own excuses as to why you have not started yet.
2. To shed light on abuse, to make it everyday conversation, so that it is less stigmatized, and consequently less rampant. Let us shed light on this problem, in all its forms.
3. Entertain you with some of my own nautical experiences that have made my life richer and might just make yours richer, too.

This book is dedicated to my brother.

I can thank him for so much, but the most important lesson of all was his reminder that life is short. Make your dreams happen while you have the time. Start the business. Write the book. Take the trip. Say the words, even when it is hard. Without him, I may still be aimlessly cruising through this life, awaiting the perfect time.

Today is the perfect time.

Introduction

Congratulations on taking the first step of changing your life into what you have always dreamed it should be! It is your life. I am sorry to remind you, but it is also truly short. Now is the time to pursue your true calling and share your unique gifts with the world.

Many of my guests aboard the Yankee Sunshine have found little bits and pieces of my story inspirational, and it has been difficult to put my finger on exactly what it is about my story that is inspiring. On a recent flight, I was enjoying a conversation with a random stranger (it is an affliction of mine), and he said the same thing. So, I decided to just ask him, "What is it about my story that you find inspiring?" His reply was not unique. I had heard this before. "You're so *lucky* to be doing what you love for a living!" I had heard similar words from a close friend earlier in life that I was *lucky* to travel so much.

What hits me like a rogue wave about that statement is the term 'lucky.' So, here is the thing. My luck is no different than yours. I promise. Sometimes, it is wonderful, sometimes it is epically horrifying. Luck is not the spice that made my life what it is today. (Also, I can promise you that I have plenty of mountains that I am still climbing). If I had to throw out a random guess at this spice, I would identify it as a mixture. Something like Old Bay Seasoning. In this mixture you would find a healthy dose of perseverance (stubbornness), faith, and courage. But what exactly is the recipe?

I began to contemplate this. I just wanted a way to share my avenue of success with others so that they may see the possibilities in their own lives. Then I saw a quote that hit me like a hurricane:

> *A dream written down with a date becomes a goal. A goal broken down into steps becomes a plan. A plan backed by action becomes reality. - Greg Reid*

If you are stuck wishing you had better luck, making excuses as to why your life cannot look the way you want it to, whether it be work, travel, or any other aspect that has you wishing for better, let me share this tale with you. It will make you laugh, cry, and all the feelings in between. My story was not an easy one. It is my wish that you see that even through some very dark circumstances, you too can ride the top of the wave, captain your own ship, and steer in any direction that suits you.

Welcome to the Sunshine Story. Read it. Plan. Make your life look exactly the way you want it to. The challenging work is worth it, I promise you!

PART I: A Dream Written Down with a Date Becomes a Goal

Dreams conjure up such positive vibes, don't they? If you hear someone say, 'I had a dream...,' you might prepare your mind for something pleasant. The fact is, I, (and very likely you, too), have countless dreams. We think things like, 'Wouldn't it be nice if....' Sometimes our dreams do not even have words to express them, like those things that just bring you joy and you know you want to be close to them. If you look back at your life, these 'genuine joy' pieces are typically glaringly obvious.

My favorite childhood toy was my 'Little People' green boat. That boat came with me on every camping trip, in every bath. Heavy rain or melting snow were my favorite types of weather. I would take that boat outside and pretend I was driving it through the channels of 'rivers and lakes'. The feel of the water beneath the hull brought peace and happiness to me. (Nothing has changed). As I grew a bit older, my dad had a little fishing boat that we would take out regularly. I fell in love with the feeling of the water beneath my feet and came to know this feeling as home early on. (I could not have cared less if we caught a single fish).

It is important to note that dreams change and morph as we grow and learn. Dreams worth attaching a date to are those ones that make you feel that joy. If we take the time to contemplate what genuinely brings us joy, and actively work to seek it out and make it an integral part of your life, you cannot help but be joyful!

Chapter 1: Just Try Your Best

Imagine you are a captain, hired to transport a boat all the way from the North end of Lake Huron to the South end of Lake Huron, for a client. The man has never even been on a moving boat but is excited for the adventure. The only logical time to start the adventure is after your current workday, at around 11 p.m. in full darkness. Once out of the river channel and onto the lake, the man begins to freak out, frantically waving his arms.

"Where are the headlights on this thing?!" he shouts, unable to contain his fear.

This is an actual event that occurred during the early years of my business. I can tell you the overwhelming feeling of fear he felt was much the same as when I was entering adulthood, rather than exiting the river channel. Don't we all wage a war with fear as we pass through new encounters in life? On my bathroom mirror, written in dry-erase marker is the passage I remind myself of daily:

The Lord has not given us a spirit of fear, but of POWER and LOVE and SOUND MIND. 2 Timothy 1:7

I felt for him. I know that feeling of fear well. As the captain of the ship, I patiently explained the radar and GPS systems, as well as the backup systems in place if those were to fail. I was able to reassure him! *We are safe, even in this unknown*

"Welp, I guess this is it...," I awkwardly shuffled into my parent's dining room, as the faces at the table glanced up at me in expectant silence. I had decided to move in with my boyfriend that summer. I could *feel* the pressing weight of their disapproval. Like any good 17-year-old, I was certain that I had laid out my life path in a way that I could survive out there in 'the wild'. Besides, it was abundantly clear that this unexpected little miracle (me) needed to break free so they could sell the house and even possibly divorce.

I was confident that this decision was best for ALL of us. On the day of my high school graduation, I packed all my belongings into black plastic bags and into the back of my car. It felt strange, knowing I was leaving all I was comfortable with behind and stretching out into my new life.

Seeing that I was most certainly shaky at best, my sister-in-law chimed in, "For what it's worth, I think you are making a big mistake." I had always felt a connection with her, and this one sentence hit below the belt, the sense of disloyalty from her stung. Looking back, I realized it was a desperate attempt to stop the wheels in motion. With the cocky confidence that comes with nearly every teenager, I stood my ground.

"On that note, I'm out," the stubborn gleam in my eyes set on my decision. "Shit. A little support would have been nice," I thought as the door clicked behind me. It was my graduation day. From high school, from home, from all things that I knew as safe.

14

Drawing a long, shaky breath, I turned the key in the ignition and rumbled down the driveway. As it turns out, my sister-in-law was spot-on. I happened to be driving into the abyss. These are the moments that we remember in our lives as very clearly **BAD** choices, but they all lead us to where we are today.

During the journey from my parents' home to Chad's, my attitude had changed from melancholy to excitement for this new adventure! Wheeling into his driveway, the first of many disappointments met me immediately. He was grumbling about something, and this simple act was one I would grow to fear.

Dismissing that, I cheerfully shouted, "Honey, I'm home!" His dismissive grunt instead of the welcoming arms I envisioned had me feeling as unwanted as ever. It was a horrible feeling, but not one that was unusual to me at that time. I wandered into the house that just yesterday he had been excited to welcome me to. He followed me in, watching me lug the heavy plastic bag into the house. The melancholy was returning rapidly.

The thoughts began to swarm into my head, "What the hell? Should I just go? But he said he wanted me here. He will be nicer later, just like he has been before. But DAMNIT, this is an excessively big day for me! It's ok, I can handle anything. I can make this work. I will work my ass off and barely be here anyway. He said he loved me. How can I face going back home? I cannot add to the chaos there. I made my bed, and I am just gonna have to make the best of this."

Working what I refer to as 'in spite of' him, I grabbed the rest of my belongings from my car and brought them in. I could tell from this early on that helping this guy be optimistic was looking like a full-time job of its own. Chad was still outside, and the air was full of an energy that hits you worse than a fist. It had grown dark outside, and I ambled to the bedroom and sat down on the bed, weary of the emotional mess of the day.

"What in THE FUCK are you *doing?!*" This was not the first lick of fear I had from hearing his voice, nor would it be the last. I frantically searched my brain for what I could have possibly done wrong. Nothing, I was drawing a blank.

He stormed in, in a fit of rage, flicking the light switch on. He stood over me, shaking with rage and cussing a blue streak. I had sat down right on a mirror that was full of lines of cocaine. Well shit. I realized quickly that I was in way over my head. His words bounced off me, as I stood wondering just how deep I had gotten myself. I did not even know he did cocaine! What else was I missing? Later, he would assure me that that was a fluke, he didn't actually do it, and that he was keeping it for a friend. (Riiighttt).

This was only the second time I had ever even seen cocaine, and I knew enough to know it was expensive. Dusting off my pants, I apologized profusely and scurried away from his anger.

The one thing my brother Mick told me during my teenage years that stuck hard was "Never let me hear that you even *tried* cocaine." I trusted that man with every fiber of my being. More than just a brother, he was my hero. I was 5 when he went away to the Air Force, hardly old enough to know who he was, but when he returned – it was magical! He was my big brother, the one that would take me for rides around our local racetrack and let me have all his hot wheels. He was *so cool,* and I knew without any doubt that his advice was GOLD. You know, there are some things in this life that you know are SOLID, and Mick was my solid.

More determined than ever that this was just a short-term fix in life, I began diligently snapping up jobs. I decided I was going to just work as much as I could to avoid dealing with Chad's attitude. I would worry about what was next when the time arose. That summer was an exhausting one, I was genuinely happy for a half day off. I worked as a clerk at a gas station during the early morning hours, straight to a hotel to clean rooms, then off to my most lucrative position- waitressing in the evening hours. I was very effectively able to have the bare minimum of contact with Chad during that summer and considered that a win. The times we were together were just for the bedroom.

It was after one of those shifts that the first time he let his anger slip into physical abuse happened. I was late returning home, and he would know as he kept tight tabs on my whereabouts. I took a chance and visited with a friend from work on my way. When I got home, he was in the shower.

In a cheerful mood, I shouted out a greeting upon arrival. I could hear the shower running, so I skipped back to the bathroom. By now, I was accustomed to judging the feel of the room. I do not know another way to describe it, but the vibe was off in a way that had my senses screaming danger, my body tense, and the lump in my throat growing.

"Hey," I tentatively whispered. He flicked back the shower curtain, grabbed the front of my shirt lifting me from the floor, pressing his fist to my throat.

"Where the fuck have you been?" he demanded, little bits of spit spraying my face, water dripping onto the floor.

Immediately, I felt guilty. I had not done a thing wrong, but that good old Catholic guilt was what rushed to the surface in this interrogation. I was terrified. I still am. By this point in the relationship, I knew the pattern. Anger, apologies, and love bombing. In that moment, I knew I just needed to get to the next step fast before he left marks.

"Just visiting a friend," I replied, not knowing that he had a friend of his keeping 'tabs' on me. His anger and my desire for the next step in the cycle to begin (STOP the fear!), led *me* to apologize, smooth things over.

Why would I be visiting a friend unless I was planning to sleep with them, right?! (Insert heavy sarcasm here).

The following day I was cleaning rooms in the hotel contemplating what I had done with my life thus far. I was wondering what I had in store for my future, and it was not at all encouraging. Looking at a coworker, a middle-aged housekeeper that was vocally unhappy with her life, I decided at once that *THIS* would not be me. I would investigate the community college and see what it would take to begin. Not to see *if* I could do it, but *how* I could make it happen. Determination was the name of my game. Still is.

After completing the application and fumbling my way through the paperwork mountain, I was on my way! I decided to take up psychology. I felt like my nature for helping others would be at peace with this choice. I tromped right up that mountain of college, my only support coming from the man whose actions prompted that choice. When I say support, I mean that in a way that I had become accustomed to at that time. The support was more like him giving me reasons to stay in college, anger, jealousy, general meanness.

When I told him of my goals and that I had landed on a psychology major, his reply, "*YoU WiLL NeVeR ChAnGe ThE WoRLd.*" For the record, this one statement has been my fuel for life. I can thank him for this.

When I changed to education (to earn his approval?), his reply, "Those who can, do, those who can't, teach."

Deciding that he would never be satisfied, and that at least teaching would keep me as busy as I wanted to be, I decided on a teaching degree. I used the rationalization that I could pour myself into this profession and avoid 'home' as much as possible. I graduated magna cum laude with my teaching certificate and was positively proud of my accomplishments during my college years!

When I landed my first teaching job, I was ecstatic. The moment I began to realize that Chad was not as happy with this accomplishment was the morning my professional career took the place of his needs. Due to multiple drunk driving violations, he had not had a driver's license for over 10 years, nor any desire to obtain one thanks to his chauffeur (me). One particular morning, he needed a ride to his ice shanty, and I needed to be at school by 7. He was well aware of my schedule, as I had been doing it for months by this point. Deliberately slow, he demanded a ride to the lake, knowing full well I would be late. In retrospect, he was definitely forcing me to decide what was more important. I was late. I made up an excuse about the cold and my car to the principal, but knew this entire situation was not getting better.

By now, I was rolling with the punches, used to the fact that I had made this choice, and the knowledge that I could make the best of it. The teaching career afforded me the opportunity to escape my prison at least five days a week. The added bonus was keeping my mind busy. This allowed me to passively ignore the abuse that was invading my personal life, seeping like poison into the crevice of every thought and action that I took.

I bet you are wondering WHY oh WHY didn't I just leave? So many people wonder about this. Even I did at times, about other abuse victims that wore their wounds as bruises. I can answer that too. Abuse is pervasive. It changes your thoughts about who you are, where you are going, and how to SURVIVE. This survival attitude becomes the modus operandi of the victim's (I HATE THAT WORD! PLEASE NO PITY) life.

Abuse permeates every aspect of a person's thought process. A simple idea to take the kids to the park becomes a matrix of thoughts, analyzing it to death to avoid the wrath of the abuser. Furthermore, the pessimistic and invalidating words from an abuser can become like truth in your own brain-forcing you to question yourself. These neuropathways become habits, and habits are difficult to break. While one is involved in the cycle of abuse, it is extremely difficult to arrive at the metacognitive point where you can see what is happening and take the exceedingly difficult steps to end it. This cycle is often referred to as a 'trauma bond.' The fact that a plethora of educational tools are at our fingertips is certainly a step in the right direction to putting an end to the cycle of abuse. Keep in mind that many victims are terrified to even research these topics on their phones. Getting caught by the abuser would bring on a rage that would prevent an escape.

I have three of the most amazing young men to prove that this was the path I was meant to take. They remind me daily of the good that can come from any situation. As with every instance in life, you learn from every situation; what **to** do or what **not to** do. They were able to glean the good parts of what their father had to offer and reject the rest. Those young men are the picture of strength and compassion!

Chapter 2: The Wind is Picking Up

After settling the client into his berth, as comfortable as my words could make him, I returned to the helm, settling in alongside my co-captain.

"The wind is picking up...we will need to track a little to the North to offset the current," he states with some concern.

"Roger that, get some rest. I've got this. The client is asleep," I report.

As the wind steadily increases, the owner returns to the bridge, his face etched with a look of genuine fear.

"Are we going to be all right?" He quietly asked.

"We are in tumultuous waters, but are headed for calmer seas," I replied, pointing at the GPS, and explaining how the land would block our wind soon.

If only our lives had a GPS to assure us that we were headed for safety soon. At these points, we just need to remember to have faith.

"Fear not, for I am with you" Isaiah 41:10

Like it or not, this was the life I chose for myself, and I would damn well make the absolute best of it. Fully in love with my teaching career choice, I worked long, fulfilling hours making sure the students had the best possible educational experience. My goal was to be sure they felt that lust for learning that would carry them through successful lives. At some point along the way, I realized that I would love to have some children of my own.

"So... I am thinking I would like to start a family. I want to be married one year before conceiving, so it looks like we are going to need to get married soon, or not. I am ok either way." My breath whooshed out after the words.

I was seriously ok either way. We had talked about marriage before, and I just could not seem to make myself do it. Now that I was CERTAIN I wanted children, I knew marriage was the next step as a 'good Catholic' girl. If it were not with him, I did not care, there were other men that would want to start a family, and at almost 27, the clock was ticking. My only concern was that another man might be *worse* than him. Looking back, I realize how awful this sounds. I had not taken the time to reflect and heal that childhood trauma and was still relying HEAVILY on that little voice in my head that whispered, "its ok, you can handle anything."

"Ok, I will call the pastor friend that I know and ask him to officiate," he replied. "We can do it next weekend."

When we told his mom of the plan, she sent a side-eyed glance in my direction, "I hope you guys can make it." He was often mean to his mom, in front of me. These times made me HUGELY uncomfortable, as though I was complicit in the verbal attacks and intimidation.

I can remember the weird combination of excitement and sadness that I could not quite name. *This was how it worked? What about love? The love I felt from him ALWAYS came after the tornado. Did everyone have this kind of life? Surely not. But maybe. Maybe I was too sensitive. Maybe I did not deserve the happily ever after proposal/wedding/romance. Maybe making sure he did not blow up was what a 'good wife' does. I could be a 'good wife.' Like everything else in my life, I put forth every bit of effort. (Just 'doing my best').*

We got married in the pastor's backyard, our 'honeymoon' a trip on our boat, per my request. He was unhappy, swallowing Pepto Bismol with frightening regularity. I could not determine if it was sea sickness or nerves. Either way, I was feeling unwanted again. That little voice in my head was whispering, "it's ok, you've got this." The truth is I *did* have it. But that is not how normal relationships work. Two people have it *together.* Thanks, therapy.

I found out I was pregnant with our first son on the same weekend we found out Chad's mother had passed. I was excited to become a mother, determined to make sure that my son would have the best chance at everything I could manage to provide for him. I was utterly convinced that my husband would mature for the sake of his own child. By the time I was 9 months pregnant, it was apparent that my husband's main concern was that our child did not interfere with my duties as a 'good wife.' I am not sure why (after the "you'll never change the world" statement), but I had assumed he would be just as excited to give our son the best start in life.

Sitting at the stoplight, the song blasting through the radio was apropos to my emotions. Not my typical genre, but "Wide Open Spaces" made me half smile with the irony...yes, I definitely needed room to make the BIG mistakes, and I hit the nail square on the head. My son wiggled in my belly, ready to make his appearance any day.

With all the rosy, positive-outlook attitude that I have become known for, I decided that I had "made my bed and now I'd have to lay in it," or at least make the best of a sticky situation. This spurred me to complete the "perfect family" with two more boys within the span of five years. When I was pregnant with our second son, I was still teaching half days at our local school. It made sense, financially, for me to work while he stayed at home with our oldest. Until the day I returned home to feel the tense atmosphere and the frantic crying of my son.

"This fuckin kid wormed his way out of the highchair and fell right to the floor," he sneered at me upon my arrival home. He began to spew excuses about his whereabouts, and I don't even remember what else as I picked up my crying son. My only goal was to reassure my baby that he was *good* and safe and that I was not mad at him. I never dreamed in a million years that Chad would have the capacity for physical abuse of an *infant,* but now I was not so sure. I decided at that moment that I was done teaching. I could not leave my baby alone with an unpredictable monster.

I sold my vehicle, learned to make my own laundry soap, grow our own food, and mourned the loss of the lessons for the babies I would no longer be able to afford on my husband's income. (He hadn't worked in a very long time, living off an accident settlement from his late teen years). I threw myself into motherhood with the enthusiasm that I was and still am known for. By the time our third and final son was born, I had decided to homeschool the three of them to give them the best possible life opportunities, and to avoid the potential discovery of my husband's secret life.

Quickly absorbed into homeschooling life, I passionately devised lesson plans to keep those boys excited about learning new things. We would have "sun" days instead of our peers' "snow" days and skip on the best days and take field trips to local preserves. My favorite days were the "pack it all up" days. We would take all the books and writing utensils necessary out to the boat, do the work while riding upriver, and go scuba diving and swimming together in Great Lake Huron.

27

Any excuse to remove us from the house was VALID if he was around. His negative nature could hardly dampen our educational adventures if we were not around. He would sneer remarks about how 'awful' the boys were and how I was most certainly cheating on him, but we were not privy to that if we were not in the home with him. It was returning home after an adventure that was becoming more frightening.

"You don't think I know where you've been?" Chad bellowed as I opened the car door. I absolutely HATED it when he was home when we returned home. You just never knew what you were going to get, but as the years passed, the odds were overwhelmingly in the favor of fear, panic, and apprehension. The boys and I had baked muffins for the local old-folk's home that morning and had just returned from joyfully passing them out to the residents.

"You think you can just whore around and I won't know?" He was bellowing at me near to the car now. By this time, I had all three unbuckled from their car seats and shooed them inside. I knew what was coming and I did not want my sons to be a witness to it, for a million reasons. (Also, when does a homeschooling momma have time to "whore around"? Asking for a friend). As he was berating me, my oldest slipped from the house, fear evident in his eyes. He was coming to "save" me.

That moment changed the course of our lives. I could not let this be the life my boys came to see as 'normal.' The next day, I started looking for a place for us. I had NO idea how I would be able to afford an apartment, but I was CLEAR that I could not keep this up any longer. I sat down with Chad when he was calmer and (bravely) told him of my plan to leave with the boys if he did not actively see a doctor and change his behavior. I was done being afraid. (Or so I thought).

To his credit, he saw a doctor, got some medication, and changed. It lasted approximately a month and a half.

As it turns out, the man you meet is actually who he will always be, not the version of him you have in your dreams. I was *certain* that he would want to be the best version of himself for fatherhood, despite OBVIOUS behaviors otherwise. His volatility was (still is) well known.

Gahhhhh, if I would have only LISTENED to my friends and family. Sometimes, my stubborn self is a bit of a problem. That same perseverance had me thinking I would make sure this little family would come out on top, whole and complete-not a statistic. God laughs at our plans, but his are SO much better.

The thought that this was my life for the next 80 years or so brought on a depression deep inside...an uncomfortable niggle that ultimately saved our lives. Rather than sinking into depression, my mom's advice of "just do your best" filtered in through my mind for the millionth time since I was 7 years old.

In the thick of it, as the abuse began to explode, I subconsciously began to devise a plan to save my children and myself. This plan was formed through years of perseverance, dotted with miracles that even an outsider has trouble believing (unless you have been right there with me).

The dream of an intact family was disintegrating and morphing into a goal of a healthy home life for my sons. The dream of being on the water in some way never left me. That is the thing about your goals. They are not static. Learning to roll with the punches is a necessary component. It was at this juncture that my main goal was to lead my boys to safety and help them have as 'normal' of a childhood as I could personally provide.

PART II : A Goal Broken Down into Steps Becomes a Plan

How do you know when to make a plan? Especially in this world that is so busy, so *complicated,* how do you know when the dream is solid enough to pursue? It is that thing you keep returning to. You know the one. Even with the chaos surrounding your life, if you pay attention, you will know.

I know I love being on the water. I know I just feel more alive when I am near to the water. It was this realization, this fact that was guiding my actions all along! When I was happiest, I was on a boat. When I was at my lowest, I would seek out the water, preferably big water (as in, the Great Lakes or the Ocean). In the background, my mind was always grinding, trying to find a way to make all the puzzle pieces fit. I love being around the public. I love the water, I love helping others learn new things, and I had been hearing that our local waterway system was "underutilized" for so long that it had just become a community mantra.

"Why doesn't someone do something?" was the community chant.

When my mind developed a solution that would connect so many puzzle pieces, I knew I had it! From this point on, it was simply a matter of connecting the dots to pave the path to execute my vision. I made the phone calls, spent countless hours researching comparable businesses, and asked the questions.

Chapter 3: The Fog

Once the client had settled in, the lake calmed down while we were heading south. It became *too* calm. The fog rolled in, thick and soupy. I headed toward the bow to wipe the window down, so that we could try and keep a sharp eye out. It was no use. We couldn't even see the front of our own boat.

Wandering up from his cabin, the client wiped the sleep from his eyes and exclaimed, "Well, now its daylight, and we still cannot see a thing!"

"We will just keep pressing forward, slow the engines, and have faith in our equipment," we assured him.

A plan to get through the apparently unnavigable waters is imperative, each step counts.

Isaiah 42:16 I will lead the blind by a way they do not know.

"Mommy, are there such things as monsters?" My youngest whispered with a trembling voice. I had gone to tuck him in and say our prayers together. This sweet little boy. How my heart ached for him. Laying there in the dark, looking for my reassurance that he would be okay. That night had been particularly hard in our home. Chad came home early and angry.

"Sweetie, the only real monsters are mean people," I replied, fighting back tears, "Don't worry, you are strong, and the good guys win!"

The escape began with a job. When it became obvious to me that change was not in the cards for the home-life situation, despite literally praying on my knees for change, I began to actively seek a viable way out. My youngest son's 4th birthday was coming right up, and I knew at a soul level that it was time. The boys were old enough to escape to the woods if things got violent while I was gone, and I knew waitressing was the fastest way to make the most money while being gone from them the least amount of time possible. If I could land a dinner shift, they would be sleeping for the most part while I made the money we needed to start over. I'd waitressed before, and knew I could handle it. The real trick was to get my then husband to agree to it. I hadn't had a job in the six years that I was either pregnant or nursing.

"So, I see that they're hiring at the Dixie," I mumbled quickly, trying to sound as casual as possible. As if the boys and my life did not depend on it.

"You can't really expect me to say you can work there," he scoffed. "That place is a meat-market. No way in hell."

"That might be how you remember it, but now it is a nice restaurant," I had done my research. The place had changed considerably over the years. "How about we go have a meal there and you can see for yourself?"

The car ride to the restaurant was quiet. So quiet, I wondered what fresh hell he had brewing for me. I pasted on my "waitress face" and said, "This should be fun! We can meet the manager and see if he is still hiring. You can see for yourself that this place is not as bad as you remember."

After we were seated, I asked our server to send the manager over when he had a moment so I could introduce myself. Chad was wary and (always) angry, but I was determined to make sure this was a positive experience.

Several days later, he finally acquiesced and said that I could work there. We were getting behind in bills and it made sense, at least until he received his next annuity payment.

After a few phone calls and basically begging for the job, the manager relented and hired me. I had not waitressed in about 8 years and I was slightly nervous about that fact. The first night I worked, I made $17 and came home to his wrath and a heavy heart. My coworkers assured me that this was going to improve exponentially in less than a month. (Boy, did it!)

This was a delicate balance. While I was away at work, the boys endured the most of his wrath, a fact that I had great difficulty reconciling. In true "Jenn" form, I made the best of it! If I was not at work, I was up early, getting us out of there on little day trips. We would make it back home in exactly enough time for me to prepare for work and go, oftentimes to the sound of my boys crying, "Please mom, don't go..." Their pleas only fueled my determination to pave a better path for them. Fear was a constant in my home and life, and I was determined not to let fear dominate the boys' lives.

My coworkers had seen it all before and quickly became like family to me, advocates.

"Tell me what advice you have on getting a divorce," I asked Jess. I was weary and the path was obvious.

"Well, first thing you will need is at LEAST five thousand dollars saved up," she replied matter of factly. "Don't even attempt it without that. Also, keep records of the abuse, complete with dates. You will need that in court."

That felt like a mountain that was impossible to climb. But I was determined. At the end of that shift, I spoke with the managers. They were somewhat aware of my situation, but it was time to confess all of it. I was at the mercy of others, and I knew it. We developed a plan that I will forever be grateful for. My manager helped me with a safe location where I could document each day's abuse.

"Get yourself a locking safe," our longtime bartender said, "I will keep it at my place."

"If things get bad, you gather the boys and trade your vehicle for my truck, and go," our manager said, locking eyes with me. I knew I could trust them both, and what other options did I have?

"Okay, thank you so much," my breath whooshed from my lungs. I had a backup plan. *Please God, don't let me have to use it.* What they offered was so much more than a backup plan. It was a feeling of support. Of love. I began to feel less lost, and the outlook looked less impossible.

I went to my favorite place that night after work. It was (and still is) a secluded beach area that overlooks the lake with the Mackinac Bridge in the background. No one was ever there that late. I spent many nights there, alone, finding peace through the despair of not knowing what would come next.

My Dixie family included many Jamaican people. Mackinaw City area businesses hire many from the country, as well as foreign colleges, to fill the labor shortages in the area. We are the typical tourist area, positively desolate during the "off-season." They bring with them their culture that I have always found fascinating. Many of my coworkers would come on my 'day trips' with the boys, and even rare camping trips! I loved showing others our life here in this place, often taking them out on my personal boat to enjoy local lakes with my boys.

One particular day as I arrived for work, one of my Jamaican coworkers cornered me, shooing me into a private booth. Sitting across from me, she grabbed both of my hands and whispering frantically with wild eyes, she said, "Jennifer. You MUST listen to me. I had a dream last night. It was a nightmare, and you were in it," she glanced around as if someone was listening. "Your husband came here flailing and shouting and causing a scene, looking for you. He was shouting, 'If I can't have her, no one will.' He pinned you to the wall right there," she pointed towards the kitchen, "and there he stabbed you." She was breathless and terrified. I was shaken.

Shaking that experience off to make sure our customer's meals were a wonderful experience was almost impossible. "Was he coming tonight?" I wondered. I will never forget that day, and often wonder if the police stopped that scene from coming to fruition the night they arrested him.

It was at the Dixie that I met V. She was our Jamaican 'salad girl' and my confidante. She came on many of the little adventures I put together with my sons, and she shared bits of her home life back in Jamaica. So, when she asked me to make her invitations with her, I was thrilled to help!

"Jennifer, would you please come to Jamaica and be in my wedding?" V asked one evening during our clean-up time. Before dismissing this as not even possible, something told me to do it. Just go. I had gotten all our passports as a piece of my backup plan. So why not? I began to daydream of seeing Jamaica, my mind frantically wondering if *this* would be a safe place for me to hide the boys if necessary. I had never even been on a commercial airplane.

"Well, how on Earth would I enact this plan if I don't even know how to navigate an airport?" I thought to myself.

I knew when to pose the question to my then husband. By now, it was obvious. If he was drunk and it was late, not a chance. If he was stoned midday, and seemingly happy, then it was a go. My only worry was those boys. What if I left them behind and he snapped? I covered that base with my family and friends. I had a plan for someone to stop in for a visit every day and take the boys for treats. Still uneasy about that, I acquiesced. The bigger picture was our way out.

My first trip on a commercial airplane was straight out of the country, to a place that did not have running water.

"This is how I die," I thought, laying there in the dark, listening to the sounds of the area. I trusted V wholeheartedly, but this was so unexpected that I was seriously thinking that I may have gotten myself in way over my head. I thought I understood poverty. I did not. At all. I was in 'the hills' that customers at the Dixie adamantly warned me against. I had brushed them off, knowing I would rather see the *real* Jamaica anyway. Well, here I was. And here I sat wondering if I was going to leave my boys behind with that monster.

As it turned out, that one trip changed my whole life! It changed my perspective on so many levels. Over the course of five days, I went from feeling sorry for the people of the small village, to wondering how they were able to be so *happy* with so little. I brought back unique items to share with my sons, as well as stories to help them comprehend where I'd just come from.

"Ok guys, time to do your level of the dishes," I announced, after sharing the little tidbits I had brought home to share. The dishwasher had three levels, perfect for the three boys to unload.

"Moooooommmmm," they exclaimed in unison, clearly distraught that they would have to actually *work*.

I sat in awe. I had just come from a place without running water, let alone a dishwasher. How could I help my boys understand what I had only just learned? It was at this moment that I realized that I would have to bring those boys to Jamaica.

We made our own 'mission trips' to Jamaica in the following years. On one of those trips, we were teaching the village kids how to swim. While we were at the beach, a man on a tiny little rickety glass bottom boat pulled up and beached the boat near to us.

"Twenty-five dollars," he shouted cheerfully, "and you can ride da boat."

Here's the thing. I have always loved boats more than any normal individual. Granted, the boat was no more than sticks and glass barely strung together, but I can swim, so I thought, "most definitely, count me in!"

As I listened to him joyfully ramble, I wondered if maybe *I* could earn a living on a boat. The thought process had started, and I began to seek out that thought process whenever I began to feel trapped by my circumstances. Don't get me wrong, it still seemed like an impossible mountain to climb, but I just began to flirt with the 'what if' thoughts that kept popping up.

Arriving back at home, I was laying in my bed, getting ready to cruise Facebook to relax a bit. The little voice inside reminded me that if I was looking to change my life, I had to change my habits. Instead of Facebook, I began to google 'glass bottom boat for sale' then 'used glass bottom boat for sale' then 'how to start your own business.' The next day, I began to develop a business class for the boys. I had decided that we were going to make a business plan together and see if we could make it work on paper.

Even if you have a plan started it is *imperative* to expect obstacles. The obstacles I encountered next certainly tested my perseverance and grit.

Chapter 4: The Light in the Distance

"We will need to refuel soon," I murmured to my co-captain.

"I see that," he replied, "Let's plan to stop at that next safe harbor.

Taking control of the navigational unit, I punched in the coordinates to the safe harbor to refuel.

Where would we be without these safe harbors to refuel us along the way? To give us the immeasurable relief knowing there is someone out there to help us along the way? It gives us *hope*.

Psalm 107:30 What a blessing was that stillness as he brought them safely into harbor.

My eyes opened in a panic. My heart thumped wildly in my chest. I frantically tried to shake the sleep from my brain. My body froze. I could hear smashing and a long string of expletives emanating from the kitchen, just outside my bedroom. I listened carefully for any little voices that might be intertwined with the cussing. Thank God they were still in bed. It was going to be a hell of a morning; he was on a warpath before daylight. I lay awake, pretending to sleep as he crashed the bedroom door open, searching for something. My fear was changing to irritation. I was so *SICK* of being afraid.

"If I can just wait this out," I thought to myself, "he will be gone soon." That was merely wishful thinking, he had no job, so nowhere to go except outside to get his "fix." By some beautiful stroke of luck, I heard his truck fire up and leave the driveway. It was just another day in the life I needed to change.

As the boys awoke, we began to get their schoolwork underway. It was typical for Chad to be gone during the day. I did not ask where, I did not care; as long as he was leaving us alone. I cheerfully put on my 'waitress face' and pretended like the morning was not as chaotic as he tried to make it. It was becoming more and more difficult to pretend.

My oldest son sent me a sideways glance, and at that moment I *knew* he was done pretending. "I know, son. Just give me one more summer. I will make this ok, I promise." I needed the time to get our plan in place. I knew without hesitation that he would financially ruin me if he were given the chance, and I did not want my boys to live in that turmoil if I could help it.

It was not long before he was rumbling back up the driveway.

"Ok, boys, now would be a wonderful time for you to take a break! You can slip outside and play for a bit. I will call you in when it is time for more work." I quickly shooed them out the back door, expecting what my son would refer to as 'the rage monster' to enter at any moment.

"Why in the *fuck* have those renters not paid yet?" he demanded angrily, slamming the front door with menace.

I was not sure what had made him angry on this day, but it could be real or imagined, as I had come to realize over the past several years. It certainly could not be the fact that the renters were only a couple of days late.

In an effort to 'smooth the waters,' I cheerfully said, "I will drive over there and get it right now."

Hustling outside, I yelled to the boys, "I'll be right back guys!" The rental was only a couple of miles away, and I figured I would be gone about 20 minutes at the most. Those renters liked to gab, so I would have to be careful to keep it short.

Arriving back home, with an envelope of cash to deliver to him, I noticed first how quiet it was. I quickly dampened the lick of fear. I had only been gone fifteen minutes. Surely nothing could have gone wrong in that amount of time. As I wandered to the front door, I began to panic. Glass was everywhere. I shouted for the boys and was greeted with that same eerie silence. Running out the back door, I hollered for them again. I saw my oldest coming toward the house from the woods.

"What's going on, where is everybody, what happened?" The words rushed from my lips as I stood there hugging him. I could see his face was shocked and *angry.*

"Dad had a fit of rage and broke the door. We were scared so we ran to the woods and hid," he said, his voice had a surprising edge of *anger* clipped to it.

Lord, my children were terrified. I was terrified. This had to STOP.

As he always did after a fit of rage, he was nice for a few days. The trouble was that the rage was becoming more violent. His words more damaging, and indicative of serious mental illness.

Not long after this incident, my youngest son and I were on a volunteer mission trip in Florida when we received the call from David. "Hey, Jenn! I know we were talking about your son possibly opening up his own business. I have an opportunity you guys might like to take advantage of. There is this program called 'Invest Cheboygan' that would provide him the opportunity to pitch his business plan on stage and possibly win up to $20,000."

A lightbulb began to burn brightly in my soul. "David. Hear me out. I have a better idea." I began to tell him of our glass bottom boat plan, and he was ecstatic.

"What is the worst that could happen," I thought to myself. I could fail. I mentally traversed that rabbit hole briefly. Then that little voice inside reminded me that those who dare to fail greatly can ever achieve greatly. I forged ahead.

The boys and I worked in earnest on the plan when we arrived back home. I had begun to see glimmers of hope. Of a way for us to live in peace. I decided to break the news to my brother and tell him of the plan that was beginning to form. I was unsure of how to navigate this enormous change, and I had zero doubt that my then husband would turn violent, even deadly, if he became aware. I could trust my brother one hundred percent.

I drove over there in secret, praying his girlfriend would not be there. My prayers were answered, and we had a sobering discussion.

"What's up, sis?" Mick said to me, concern etching his face.

I flopped down on his couch. "Are you alone for a bit?"

"Yeah, she's gone, I don't know where, but I don't expect her back soon," he replied, sitting across from me.

"I am scared, Mick. He is getting meaner by the day, and I need to get those boys out of there," I said bluntly, swallowing the lump in my throat. Hearing the words spoken aloud killed me inside. The thoughts bombarded me. It *is* real. This is *my* life. How did it come to this? *Thank GOD* I have my brother. Please help me.

I described to him the business plan but reminded him that it was just a dream at this point, but I had reason to believe it was at least possible.

"Wow sis, I didn't realize how bad it was getting," my brother replied. Seeing the look on my face, the words he said next were words I will not ever forget. I had ALWAYS been able to count on Mick. Always. No matter where I had gotten my Jeep stuck, no matter what time of day I needed help and with anything at all, he ALWAYS said 'Ok, let's fix this.' That day was no different. I had no idea what my brother would say to this revelation, and I hated that I needed help, but he came through, as always.

He looked me square in the eyes, "Ok. You listen carefully. I understand what you are going through. We will do whatever it takes. When you are ready, just bring the boys and move in here. You are welcome to stay as long as you need to get back on your feet.

I must have sat there with my jaw dropped for five minutes. "What?" I was certain I heard wrong. "Thank you," I gushed.

"Do not worry, sis. We can make this work."

I left his home feeling more hope than I knew was possible. I had a plan. For survival, and for thriving. I knew my brother would let no harm come to us.

The intensity of the situation had not reached its height. As it turns out, it was only the beginning.

Chapter 5: Dangerous Territory

All fueled up and ready to get back underway, we carefully motored away from the safe harbor. I was exhausted and ready to take a break from straining my eyes into the fog.

"I'm going to take a little shut eye," I told my co-captain, "You've got this for a little bit?"

"Sure thing," he happily replied, "It's about time you rested."

Laying down on the bench seat, I closed my eyes and reflected on the blessing that was me on a boat on a long journey. I could not imagine a better place to rest.

"Hey, Jenn," my co-captain was shaking my shoulder, "We are entering a dangerous area, filled with shallow shoals. I'm going to need your eyes to help navigate."

Shaking the sleep from my head, I sat up, ready to face the next set of obstacles.

It is during our darkest moments that we must focus to see the light. -Aristotle

Less than one month later, my life as I knew it, would never be the same.

"Hey sis, I have some bad news. Do you remember the back pain I was telling you about?" I did remember him talking about it, I even gave him some ideas to ease it. I assumed it was because he was always working hard.

"Yeah," I mumbled with trepidation.

"I've also had blood in my urine. The doc says its kidney cancer."

NOnononononoooonononono. No. No. The urge to scream was unbearable. "Ok. We've got this. I have a homeopathic doctor that can work with that. She can heal. But you MUST follow the protocol to the letter. Tell me yes. Tell me I can do this one thing for you. She healed her own stage 4 cancer, and she can heal yours. PLEASE," I rambled uncontrollably. I did not care what I had to do. The hours I would work. The specialized foods I would prepare. We WOULD beat this.

"Just come stay here. I am begging you, just until you are healed." I felt helpless.

"Sis, I can't do that," I'm fairly certain he would not, because of my own situation. "But I will try your doctor," he said. I was elated by this news! I would help my brother beat this.

The competition for the startup money was rapidly approaching. It was almost impossible to separate the urgency for healing my brother and extricating my boys from the upheaval at home. I would spend days researching how to beat his cancer and how to perform on stage in these types of contests. All while making sure the boys were shielded from their often drunk, incredibly angry father. I could not help but feel as though my life was out of control. I was on autopilot. *Just do what I need to in order to survive.*

Finally, the big night was here. I was too preoccupied to be nervous, the stakes were too high. I was wearing my wetsuit for the presentation, and it was so *hot* backstage that I seriously regretted it. I had never been onstage before, but I just kept telling myself it would all be ok. Do not vomit, do not stress. You've got this. Practice your lines. Those mantras ran circles in my brain.

"Next up, we have Xplor Shipwrecks and More," the announcer said. My youngest son made that name up, and it was a comfort to me knowing he was in the audience hearing that. I completed my presentation as though I was born for the stage. Hardly a single hiccup. I *nailed* it. Walking off the stage, my smile was beaming. Now, I just had to await the judge's verdicts.

The other candidates and I were patiently awaiting the results while mingling with the audience. There were about three hundred people milling about, randomly coming up and offering congratulations on ideas and performances. The reception of our idea was wonderful. I had support that I was not even aware of. This simple fact would keep me pressing on when times became dark.

The announcement began with third place, and when I did not hear my name, I told myself it was okay. I wanted first anyway. Then second place, still nothing. Then first place. Nothing. It was like a punch to the gut. I put on my happy face, even though I was reeling inside. *What do I do now?*

The next day, I ran on the trail. Hot tears streamed down my face as I wondered if I was even on the right track. Was this the right thing to do? Was *anything* I was doing the right thing? How was I going to make this happen? Should I even try?

As a cradle Catholic, it was ingrained that divorce was 'wrong.' Watching my parents as I grew up was living proof that, technically, two people could stay married, for the sake of marriage. Maybe I needed to pray more. Maybe the rosary. Some little fire inside of me said 'stay the course.'

For two days, I was floundering. I was genuinely questioning everything, from every possible angle. My oldest brother once mentioned that I should have become an engineer. My ability to analyze a situation is above par. I analyzed the situation *to death*.

I was in the parking lot at the local parts store when I received yet another phone call that would alter the course of my life.

"Hey there, is this Jennifer?" the man on the other end asked after I had answered.

"Yes," I replied tentatively.

"Hey kid, I was in the audience the other night, and watched your presentation. I want to let you know that you did a phenomenal job and I commend you for that. Your business is exactly what this small-town needs, and your enthusiasm is not something I have seen in a long time," he spoke with authority. For the life of me, I could not figure out why he was calling. It was nice to hear, after a rough couple of days, but still.

"Bottom line is this: I think you have what it takes to make this thing happen. How much do you need to get the loan?" he said it with such *finality*. Here was an outsider, someone that knew nothing of the reasons for my drive to make this happen, believing it could happen. Believing *I* could make it happen.

Leaving the driveway of the parts store, I could not contain my ear-to-ear grin. My mind was racing a million miles an hour. Holy smokes. My life would never be the same and I knew it down to my core. The excitement was surreal. The belief that I was on the right track was just solidified. I turned the music up and sang along...I was just going to bask in this feeling for the ride home, at least. For once, I just settled into the victory, simply for its enjoyment. This weird little roller coaster called life was back on the upswing. I just needed to remember to have some faith.

I cruised over to my brother's house to tell him the big news.

"You are looking like you're feeling much better!" I exclaimed as I took my first look at him.

"Really?" he said, misery all over his face, clearly wishing this were true.

The thing is it was true. He did look like he was on the upswing. The meals and supplements were doing their job. I had every reason to hope this was going to all be OK!

"My latest test results are in. I just got off the phone with the doctor. The tumor on my kidney has increased in size by a third." The look on his face was a look of pure defeat.

I know you are not supposed to hate, but at that moment I HATED that doctor for stealing hope from my brother. I was going to have to work so much harder.

Arriving back at home, the boys and I had a meeting. (The soon to be ex-husband was gone-as usual). I explained what was happening with their uncle. Remembering the offer from the private investor like a revelation, I explained how amazing this opportunity was, and how hard we were all going to have to work. The boys' somber attitudes had me concerned.

"What's going on here?" I asked with concern etching my voice. They knew that their uncle's health had me sad, but their vibe was off in a big way.

It was then that the boys began to release all the details of the latest of the 'rage monster' tantrums that had happened while I had been in town. Apparently, he had come home long enough to terrify the boys and then left again. I listened, explained for the millionth time that that was not how grown men should act, and calmed them down.

"Boys," I began, looking each of them square in the eyes as I spoke, "one more summer. If we can make it through one more summer tip toeing around him, I will have a better life for us. I *promise*."

We decided it would be a fabulous homeschool adventure to bring the boat home up the Mississippi. The boys and I would be out of the house for several weeks that summer, making life easier for all.

The boat would be built in Slidell, Louisiana. I was prepared to have it shipped to the upper Mississippi where we would meet it and have the adventure of a lifetime. I had asked around for advice, and found a retired, well-seasoned captain willing to come along as a 'Mississippi River Guide.'

I began to go about my life with more confidence and determination than ever before. There are a couple of things that my stint onstage accomplished: the business plan was in motion, and I was now somewhat of a public figure in our small town. This might not seem like much, but when you are considering divorcing a dangerous man, it helps to know that many other people know who you are and are watching for you. It helps to keep you alive.

CHAPTER 6: Navigating the Course of Shoals

"**This** is a mess!" I exclaimed, wondering just how accurate the depth of the water was on the navigational chart.

We were threading our way through the area of shoals, trying to steer clear of the rocky outcroppings that would annihilate our vessel, should we encounter them.

Glancing at the radar, I saw a return on the screen that could only mean a looming freighter.

"We are going to want to keep the course closer to the shore," I said to my co-captain.

"Why?" he replied, "What are you seeing over there?"

"There is a freighter off the port side bow," I replied, "We should be past it in a few minutes."

We were exhausted. The way was challenging, but we were confident in our skills to make it through.

The most difficult thing is the decision to act; the rest is merely tenacity. -Amelia Earhart

I flopped down on my brother's bed, "Mick, come on, open your eyes! The bank called and they need me to name this boat that isn't even built yet. I brought you a smoothie, will you please try and eat some?" I chirped brightly. I made it my mission to bring him cheer every single day.

He nodded his head slowly. Watching your best friend/hero in this world die right before your eyes is a special kind of hell that I would not wish on anyone. I spent countless hours preparing food that he might find palatable, yet still in the confines of the zero-sugar diet. The homeopathic treatments only work if you follow them to the letter. I saw an empty M & M wrapper on his bedside. I knew I was fighting a losing battle. With so many obstacles to overcome, I relented and just tried my best to help him know just how much I loved him.

He was rapidly losing the ability to speak, in fact, my visits were just long monologues about my day. (And me silently begging him to get better.)

He croaked out the first words I'd heard from him in days, "ccc-rrrassshhh."

A laugh escaped my lips, "Nice. Thanks," I added sarcastically, "That'll give me LOTS of customers."

I really wanted that from him. For him to name my boat. That man gave me the courage to do so many things in my life, and this new adventure was no exception. We (me, because the conversations were mainly monologues) decided on 'Yankee Sunshine,' as those were two things I had been called my whole life. Yankee because I really like to drive fast, and Sunshine because of the sunshine in my personality.

The cheery façade left my demeanor as soon as I closed his front door. I climbed in the Jeep and just sat there in the driveway, numb. The rage bubbled up inside me from nowhere. I turned the key in the ignition and Metallica came thumping through the speakers. I cranked that volume until it would give me no more. I had to drown out the pain in my head. The music seemed to be giving me a break and getting a little louder. As if from a fog, I realized it was me making that noise, a primal scream that came right from my soul.

Driving the five miles between his house and mine, I came to the place in my head that would enable me to survive the next year. Whenever life is impossible, like really too much, you must lie to yourself a little. Just tell yourself that it's really not that hard and that you can do anything. If you're going through hell, keep on moving.

Arriving home that day, I glanced around at the peaceful winter snow and decided to just take a break. I could feel the blessing. Grabbing the sleds, I yelled for the boys and headed for our back property. Whizzing down a hill at ridiculous speeds on a little plastic disc sounded like a perfect way to stay in the moment with them. My goal of having them maintain stability in this shite show felt like an uphill battle of epic proportions.

At work the following evening, I was able to take a breath. Helping others seemed to be the perfect way to escape my own bit of trauma. I was blessed to genuinely have the ability to listen to other's concerns and actually offer useful advice. I had been doing that for years as a server, and it helped me as much as my customers. I went to 'my beach' that night and let the tears escape.

The following morning was another story altogether. I awoke to what was rapidly becoming 'the usual.' Crashing dishes, cussing loudly, the angry vibe ripe in the air. One would think that waking up to this so often would calm the nervous system a bit-simply because you would be used to it. You never get used to it. It is always terrifying. Only now, it was also becoming annoying to me.

I tip-toed from the bedroom to confront the madman.

"You'd better get that little fucker to apologize to me," Chad spewed from his mouth. His crazy eyes had me spooked. (All this before 8 a.m.). He continued to ramble angrily about how awful this person was, how stupid and mean and all manner of things.

 I couldn't tell who he was talking about, so I finally interjected, "WHO?!"

At this point, he shouted right back the name of our oldest son. He was fourteen years old. To say I was livid is perhaps the most grandiose understatement of the century. The mama bear was pissed.

Controlling my urge to match his angry energy and direct it back at him, I calmly made a decision. My head was swirling. This was the wakeup call I needed. There is literally nothing any human could have done to endure his mountain wrath that morning, let alone his own son.

"I will talk to him," I mumbled, on autopilot.

"See that you do," he sneered.

"I said I would. That's ENOUGH," I growled back at him. The look I must've had on my face shut him up. He had gone too far. It was one thing to treat me like this, but I would not allow this to happen to my children.

I walked down the hallway, into my son's bedroom. To my astonishment, he was not in his bed. Walking back, I caught a glimpse of him in my bed, hugging my pillow and sobbing uncontrollably into it. He had heard everything. The look on his face as he glanced up, prepared to defend himself, broke my heart.

"Mom, I..." he was quickly trying to tell me 'His side.'

"Shush, oh my boy," I hugged him tightly.

"Mom, I don't care what we have to do. Just get him out of here, please," he rambled with misery all over his face.

I grabbed his shoulders and looked him square in the eyes. Using my thumbs to swipe away his tears, I said to him, "Don't you worry about a thing. We've got this. He will be gone. Now wipe your tears and get ready for church." We all went to church that morning. One big 'happy' family. I was done living the lie. My children were done suffering the consequences.

CHAPTER 7: Moving Ahead

"**Why** are we moving so slow?" demanded the client, after he stumbled up the stairs to the bridge. He was drunk, having been tipping the bottle all night long. He was becoming belligerent, a definite issue when the captain's attention must be focused on maintaining peace.

"Hey, they're doing the best they can," his buddy said, coming up to the bridge to try and coax him into calmness. This was the same guy that kept giving him the alcohol last night.

My co-captain and I shot each other a weary glance. Just when you think you have everything under control, another monkey-wrench gets thrown into the mix.

"My Glock is in the front zipper of my large duffel in the galley," he murmured to me, when the two were out of earshot. I just nodded; thankful he had thought to bring one.

Traversing the shoals was a long and arduous process, when combined with the heavy fog and looming freighters. Thankfully, the client and his friend had drunk themselves into a stupor, too drunk to really irritate either one of us. We had to be on our 'A' game to be assured safe passage.

Sometimes, your 'A' game means simply moving forward. Even if the movement is slow and careful, it is forward.

All dreams are within reach. All you have to do is keep moving toward them. -Viola Davis

The day my brother passed from this world I went to work at the restaurant. You read that right. I had nothing else to do, nowhere else to go. I had gotten the phone call while I was preparing for work, I already knew it was coming. Some things you just know.

"Jenn? He's gone," my sister breathed the words into the phone.

 I crumbled into the corner of my bedroom and curled up into a little ball of misery. I am unsure of how long I sat there. My then husband was not home, and I had never been more thankful for that one fact. Swiping at my face, I put on some resolve and swallowed the lump in my throat. I called the boys into my bedroom, told them the news, they too knew it was coming. No surprises there. My body began to shake and never stopped for three days. It was like a vibration I could not control no matter how hard I focused.

I called the shift manager at work, "Hey Laura," I said, my voice sounding foreign to my own ears, "my brother has passed. I will be coming into work, but please just tell everyone not to ask or talk to me at all about it." Auto-pilot was what I needed that night. One foot in front of the other.

Oddly, work went fine despite the funny little tremors that my body had. I had an ever-present bottle of Tums to settle my stomach. By the end of the shift, I had no idea what to do next, so the emotions came bubbling up to the surface. I sat with my work family in a booth after the patrons had long since gone. They offered words of comfort, and for their patience with me that night, I am indebted. I sat at my beach for hours after midnight, letting the water heal me.

It is worth noting that I had no idea how to proceed in those months. The death of my brother, the looming divorce, the starting of a business were all foreign to me. My life was a real-life version of 52 pick-up and the definition of chaos. Every day I woke up in prayer that God would direct my path and keep us safe. Little miracles kept me sane throughout that process.

One of those miracles came from a friend from my high school days.

"Jenn, I have a boat you might be interested in for dive charters," Jeff said. He knew my passion for water and diving and was present in the audience when I was onstage asking for startup money. I had some money saved. It was not much, but he was asking for a price well below the boat's value, and after a conversation or two, I was convinced I could multiply that money with the help of the boat. The simple *kindness* offered humbled me while my life was in shambles.

I began to take this new project on with gusto. I was waitressing while awaiting the production of the Yankee Sunshine, and this seemed like a perfect fit to add to my bank account to be sure I could pay those big boat payments when it arrived. I understood my first year in business would be squeaky tight, financially.

Things at home were even worse than before. My then husband's violent behavior was escalating, and every day was a delicate balance to 'keep the peace.' I kept putting one foot in front of the other. The promise I made to my oldest son less than a month prior was on my mind every day.

I happened to be walking past the server station when I noticed my phone ringing. It was my neighbor.

"Hey Jenn, Chad just drove past here several times, driving erratically. I am quite sure he is drunk. Are you ok?" Penny sounded worried. I had a full section at the restaurant, so I quickly thanked her and affirmed that I was ok.

"Can you please drive to my house and 'pop' in to be sure the boys are not with him?" I asked her.

She called back within moments to report that the boys were all home, unawares and safe. I tried to finish my shift but begged off early. The shift manager was aware of my situation, and the dream of my Jamaican coworker was at the forefront of my brain. We all were keeping an eye out for Chad's truck outside as we worked. Once again, I had no idea what to do. I sat down heavily in the chair at the server station. I did not want to go home until he passed out. I wanted my boys protected, but maybe he would be ok if he did not see me. I was a trigger for his violence.

At that moment, my phone rang again. It was an unknown caller. I picked it up and answered with confusion, "Hello?"

"Is this Jennifer?" the officer asked.

"Yes," I replied.

"We are in the process of arresting your husband. He is resisting. There is a dog in the truck, can you get the dog?" the officer stated.

"Oh, thank God, yes. I can." I was so *relieved!* He would be in jail. This was his fifth DUI. He would be there for a long time, with any luck.

That night I had to explain to my boys what was going on. The next morning, I took them to the store to pick out phones. In my 'perfect world' parenting plan, they would have bought their own with their first job. If we were to be doing this alone, they would need to be able to communicate with me. I called the jail that morning with high hopes that were dashed instantaneously. He would be released by noon.

"How is this possible?" I thought, tears threatening. He has five drunk-driving incidents, this was a 'super drunk,' he had a loaded weapon on the front seat, and drugs in the truck. He was out in twenty-four hours?!

I personally served the divorce papers to him less than a week later, in a crystal-clear moment of 'now is the time,' despite my fears. He had the fit you would expect, only I was *done*. Done being afraid. Done watching my boys think his behavior was 'normal.' Done being treated like garbage.

Done being afraid. Little did I know that things were about to get much, much worse. Somewhere deep in my gut, I knew that would be the case. I just didn't care. Turns out that the adage 'keep your friends close, and your enemies closer' has some truth to it.

CHAPTER 8: WTF

Right about midway through the trip, the drunks began fighting down below. My co-captain and I simultaneously let out audible sighs. Sometimes life just gets so ridiculous that we have to stand there, with our mouths ajar, and just wonder 'what just happened?'

It was at this point that I just could not believe our luck. It was a most peaceful day out on my very favorite lake. Sure, there was fog and shoals, but it was calm and warming up quickly.

"Well, I guess it's my turn to go settle them down," my co-captain said, with clear resignation in his voice.

"Ok, Captain, I am all set up here," I replied, relieved I was in charge of the helm and not babysitting.

Tough times never last, but tough people do. - Robert H. Schuller

There are many reasons why abuse victims remain in destructive situations. I know this because I had several reasons of my own. Not the least of which was fear of the abuse escalating if I tried to leave. As it turns out, this is rather common and sometimes deadly. It is not a fear to be taken lightly. According to Campbell et al., 2003b; Garcia et al., 2007, "Women who were separated after living with the perpetrator were over three times more likely to be victims of homicide than those who had not been separated." The fear is founded, and I felt it through every fiber of my being.

At first, I was hopeful that it could just be a quick amicable split. I quickly realized that my fears that he would do *anything* to hurt me once he had 'nothing to lose' were spot on. What I had not seen coming was the fact that hurting our children would be included in that.

Here comes the 'Jerry Springer' version of the story. Buckle up.

Chad was ordered to leave the home on account of abusive behavior. The caveat was that he could come back on Friday-Sunday from 3-11 pm to 'babysit' the boys while I was at work. He would verbally abuse them to the point I had decided to purchase a camera to place strategically in my home to have evidence for the court system. He would throw parties on the lakefront while the boys were uncomfortable in their own space, using food I had purchased to feed us throughout the week. Later, he would tell a judge that he had been *giving* us 'food.' Not only did he *NOT*, but he also actually *stole* what we had.

Those days were long and the definition of difficult, but nothing could have mentally prepared me for the ultimate betrayal.

"I have the papers you've requested," I said, as he opened the door. It was unmistakable that I was walking in on a romantic interlude between my dead brother's 'wife' and my soon to be ex-husband. My brother had only been gone two months. And I could not believe my own eyes. In retrospect, this was just another form of abuse/punishment, but at the time I just could not believe that he/they would do that to my brother's memory. Let alone my boys and my niece.

The vicious grin from my brother's 'wife' and that of Chad let me know that my face had revealed to them that they had hit their mark. How long had this been going on? How disgusting can two people be? I am still in utter disbelief that anyone could think that would be ok on any level. The looks of pity on people's faces around town were only building my resolve. I would make sure my boys had as normal a life as I could.

My soon to be ex was a millionaire and I was dead ass broke. I was working as much as I could and worrying twice as much about the boys being in front of computers too much.

After the blessing of being on a boat for several hours one morning that summer, (captaining a dive charter), followed by a quick nap in the Jeep, and backed up by a long night at the busy restaurant earning every single tip, I collapsed into my bed. I was asleep on the way to the pillow.

For the third time in a week, I sat bolt upright, from a dead sleep. What *was* that noise? Scrubbing the sleep from my brain as quickly as I could, I listened with intent. Oh *shit*. I knew that sound. Our home was an older one. Whenever an outside door was opened the windows would 'flex,' making a whooshing sound. *Someone was either in my home currently or had just left.* It was just the boys and I in our home. There was only one person that would do this.

As I lay awake, head resting on my pillow, fighting back a wave of panicked terror, I decided that this was not going to define me. After all, my boys needed me to be strong. I got up out of my bed and tiptoed to the closet. Fumbling around, my fingers brushed the cool metal of my pretty teal Glock. I carried it with me as I went and locked every door and window. I checked on the boys and headed back to my room.

Slipping the gun beneath my pillow, I finally decided that, on this night, I would get some rest. I mentally prepared myself before closing my eyes. If it came down to it, I could do what it would take to protect us. I was tired to the bone. Not simply the exhaustion of a full day's work, but my whole *being* was weary. My spirit was in there, fighting valiantly to rise up. Scraping the walls of my internal prison with bloody fingernails, I climbed from the abyss, the light on the Yankee Sunshine shining the way. I called the manufacturer every week to check on the progress. It was going to be late. Summer is short here, and boat payments would be large.

Grinding. Always grinding. Lock the doors, save some cash, keep the customers happy, be the best momma possible, fix the damage he was doing to them, talk to my attorney. It was a summer of grinding. Head down, nose to the grindstone, you can do this, you *MUST* do this.

I had gotten into the habit of locking every single door/window a matter of routine (not the typical behavior 'up north') when I heard the doorbell ring one evening. Looking out, I saw that it was Chad. Happy with myself for remembering to lock up so he would not be able to do his usual barging right in, I went out into the garage to answer the door. Greeting him there as a roadblock to my home was one of the most frightening things I had ever done. He was an intimidating man.

"Looks like it's scary being here all alone," he jeered at me in a sing-song voice, the evil in his eyes giving away his insinuation.

"I'm not scared at all," I replied with a straight back and confidence I did not feel, "what do you want?"

In retrospect, these little moments remind me of many people describing me as fearless. I am not, nor have I ever been. What determines who a person is is what they do in the face of that fear. I have had ample practice in that department.

Up until this point, I had a worthless attorney. The ex was using the court system to further the abuse, postponing every court date on his whim. Separately, he was wiggling free of any charges from the drunk-driving incident that spring. It turns out, you get what you pay for. The soon to be ex had not given us a dollar towards any of the home expenses/food/clothing, and I had three boys to care for. Their needs had to come first.

"Jennifer, I don't care what you have to do. Get rid of that attorney and find one that can do the job right," my cousin John had heard enough. I was willing to walk away from almost everything (not my boys) and be in financial ruin if Chad would just leave us alone. He would never leave us alone was what I was learning. He would ruin me and the boys as punishment. My cousin was thousands of miles away and still gave me the encouragement and direction I needed.

I googled 'best divorce attorney' in our state, found a candidate, prayed, called, and told him my story. He agreed that he could help and told me the fees. I sucked up my pride and called my oldest brother to beg for a loan. It was a considerable sum of money, but I paid my family back as soon as the divorce was final, when he was finally ordered to pay me half of everything. It was yet another lesson for me to learn; how to receive from others. I had enjoyed giving but receiving felt extremely uncomfortable and humbling.

The day the Yankee Sunshine arrived in our town was the day hope was restored in my heart. It was late August. I knew it was coming that day, I had been in constant contact with the shipping company. I had long since given up the dream of bringing it home up the Mississippi, as the boat was late in production, and my summer had turned into the biggest hot mess imaginable.

Patience was never my signature virtue when awaiting something that I longed for. I decided to take my mind off the phone that refused to ring by taking a long swim in the lake. By the time I had toweled off and grabbed my phone, I had three missed calls. I could not get those boys gathered fast enough.

"THE BOAT IS HERE," I shouted with utter excitement in the house, "COME ON HURRY UP!"

PART III: A Plan Backed by Action Becomes Reality

When you know what your passion is, you find a way to incorporate it into your life in a way that will bring you a sustainable life both financially and spiritually. What comes next? A beautiful mixture of perseverance, faith, and courage, with some hard work sprinkled in.

Take the time to daydream it through. If others can do it, why can't you? These were my thoughts. I did not even know the first step, so I researched it. I was turned down and laughed at without a business plan. So, I researched how to do that and did it.

Next, I daydreamed about how the tours would look. I called people who knew the area even better than me, and I asked questions. I listened to those that were willing to share their knowledge. I scoured the internet and put together information that would help guide the way.

I researched all that it would take to be completely legal. I shored up my courage and called the USCG and had several hour-long talks. I humbled myself and admitted what I did not know so that I could learn what I needed.

That's just the thing. You don't even know what you need when you begin. It is all a learning process that is simply incredible. It was effective for me, and I still use this process today, in all areas of my life.

CHAPTER 9: COLD WINTER, HOT FAITH

"**Hey Jenn**, I think they're gonna be asleep for the duration of the journey," my co-captain said.

My relief was written all over my face. We had a hell of a journey even without their shenanigans. I could see that my co-captain felt the same way.

And just like that, the Great Lake settled down, the fog began to lift, the sun began to shine. I was in the company of a friend, on my favorite lake. We were close to our destination and cruised along in peaceful silence. I was reveling in the awe of the lessons we learned along the way.

To have faith is to trust yourself to the water. When you swim, you don't grab ahold of the water, because if you do you will sink and drown. Instead, you relax, and float. - Alan Watts

All along, I had prayed for so many things that I was certain God was sick of hearing from me. I prayed for safety every day and most nights, even throughout the night. I prayed the business would support us. I prayed that I would be the best mom possible under the circumstances we were dealing with. The list goes on forever. It was (and still is) a common theme in my life. I was not always a heavy pray-er, but when I was faced with literally no other choice and a larger than life mountain to climb, it turned out to be my go-to.

I had a big, beautiful boat. I had a wonderful business plan. I had (miraculously) people surrounding me with support. Still, the boat was extremely late. The tourist season would be over before I could even earn money. We had sea-trials, practice runs, and a plethora of inspections to check off the list before we could even have one paying customer.

When I say the stress of the situation was intense, know that this comes on the heels of the singular most stressful summer of my life.

"I've got this," I thought, trying my darnedest to believe myself. There had been no support whatsoever coming from my soon-to-be ex-husband. I had some money saved from waitressing and dive charters, but those boat payments were going to deplete that before Christmas. The court dates were delayed for so long that I had begun to believe that there would never be an end to this divorce. Each delay was brought to my attention by the soon to be ex via text message before any email. Those texts read, "Looks like it's delayed again☺☺." He was loving this. Using the courts to torture me as well.

Perseverance became my persona. Once the season was over, I hunkered down and began to research the details of the abuse we were enduring. It turns out that there is a pattern that is well documented of this type of abuse. I found many resources and began to employ advice gleaned from there. There were numerous accounts of people dealing with virtually the same situation. I felt comfort in knowing I was not alone. The soon to be ex's comments became a predictable series that I now had the knowledge to overcome.

No matter the dire financial circumstances, I had this gut instinct that things were going to be better. They *had* to. That feeling of fear was nothing to me anymore. Like, 'yeah, so what, it is scary. Now how do I overcome this?' It was becoming my habit. I can assure you that it was never a comfortable habit, but it was definitely a useful one. I had, (and have), a different relationship with fear than I had at the beginning of this process.

That winter, so many little miracles happened. I do not know how people knew, but they did. There are some benefits to living in a small town! One angel gave me a check randomly that covered my personal bills for one month, another community foundation gave me a grant to cover a boat payment or two, generous tippers at the restaurant gave me hope for another month. My scuba divers called and made plans for diving with me the next summer and *insisted* on making deposits.

Coming home from town with the boys to find a box of food on my doorstep caused this strange combination of feelings inside, the two most prominent were gratitude and defeat.

"Mom, why are you crying," my youngest asked me that evening. I was surprised by the comment because I didn't even realize my face was leaking.

"Oh honey, God is *so* good sometimes that it surprises me. These are happy tears. I don't know who gave us these groceries, but I am grateful," I replied, smiling. I had no idea what I was going to do that week for groceries. Some angel fixed that problem for us.

CHAPTER 10: YOU'VE GOT MOXY

My co-captain and I were peacefully navigating our way down south, both congratulating each other on our respective way of 'handling' the client and his friend, while dealing with the series of navigational hazards thrown our way.

Soon we needed to refuel again.

"Hey, I know a great little marina that we can stop at and maybe take a little walk into town and grab a bite to eat," he said. He had shuttled boats this way before and knew all the best stops.

"Sounds wonderful," I replied. I had not brought much more than a snack along, as we began this journey at the tail end of a long workday of my own.

"Who is going to alert our 'passengers'?" he said, with laughter in his eyes. We both knew that they just wanted to be at home port, as they were likely hung-over. A stubborn gleam shone in my eyes.

"I'm on it," I said, ready to take on the challenge.

When your dreams are bigger than the places you find yourself in, sometimes you need to seek out your own reminder that there is more. And there is always more waiting for you on the other side of fear. -Elaine Welteroth

With spring came work! My oldest son had decided he would help to narrate the trip, and my youngest two helped to run the 'shop,' (a little merchandise trailer we spent the winter converting to a shop). I was *ready* and not just a little bit worried. The boys and I could handle this with the help of Keith, a fellow captain and historian that had agreed to work for me that summer.

I was on my way home from visiting a friend when I received a phone call from Keith, "Jenn," he stammered, "I have taken a job at the county marina."

"I didn't realize you were even looking," I said awkwardly, fighting that all too familiar wave of panic/stress.

"I'm sorry to leave you in a lurch, but I have a friend that might be willing to help out," he said quickly, "I will give you his number. His name is Rob."

After we hung up, I took a few minutes to gather myself. I knew the feeling of stress on a molecular level. This was minor compared to the past year of my life, but the business plan I had in place for success was just altered and I needed the business to have the best employees.

I decided to make the call to Rob. When I say that was one of the most solid decisions of my life, I am not exaggerating! He happened to be a historian that loved the water and boats. (He still does, despite the propensity of the position to demand long hours). Throughout the summer, he would entertain all aboard the Yankee Sunshine with his historical stories. That switch was a blessing in disguise, like so many other things that had happened. (*When will you have faith, Jennifer?!*)

There is something to be said about having hope amid chaos. The soon to be ex had tried every single play in the book to drag out the divorce proceedings, and it was looking like one year later, the proceedings would finally begin. Just in time for my very first full summer season. What a season it was! It started out slowly, and I began to wonder if I would be short on money that winter too. Then July and August hit. What a wonderful (and exhausting) experience those two months were!

I set the schedule so that I could run the dive boat in the mornings, and the glass bottom in the afternoon and evenings. I was not out of the woods yet. I would take every opportunity to earn money that I could. I was determined not to endure another winter like the last one.

We worked hard that summer, with a bare-bones crew. I was exhausted, but this time a happy exhausted. The divorce was not final yet, but the house was peaceful. The business was looking like it was going to be a success, even though I did not take a breath until I had exactly enough money to make all the payments throughout the winter, plus a bit extra to cover springtime costs.

In addition, I had been granted a lifetime restraining order against my soon-to-be ex after he took me to court three separate times just to lift the order that was granted that winter. Every single court date was stressful and expensive, and he knew it. This is typical of post separation abuse. That piece of paper had a heavy workload over the coming months/years. He would (and still does) challenge it.

On one particular day in mid-August, the customers were just showing up for the afternoon cruise, and a sleek expensive looking car rolled up.

"Mom, this man would like to talk with you," my youngest son rushed to me.

"Ok, you take over checking people in," I replied, slightly annoyed. Why didn't the man just come and talk to me? I was obviously busy.

I walked over to the car, instantly regretting my annoyance. He was an older gentleman, and what he had to say was the truth. It was also such a blessing to hear aloud from a complete stranger that had obviously been following the business.

"You've got MOXY," he said with his eyes twinkling, "I am in awe of all that you have accomplished here and I just wanted you to know that."

It is funny how some words just stick with you. They stand out and help define who you are becoming. That day I felt self confidence that I had not felt before. I just wish I could share the feeling of utter *joy* with everyone.

My gratitude for the distance I had come over the past year was overflowing. Each trip back up the river on the Yankee Sunshine, full of guests, I would think to myself, "Thank you, God!"

That fall the divorce was *finalized!* I knew with growing certainty that the ex-husband's threats would not come to fruition. The boys and I would *not* be homeless, broke, begging him for anything. The sheer feeling of relief is impossible to convey with words.

In celebration, my cousin that had given me the sage advice a year and a half prior (get an attorney that knows what they are doing), sent me a full box of Alaskan King crab legs, overnight, straight from his town in Alaska. We decided to use that box of crab legs to throw a terrific party to give proper thanks to all the people that I consider miracles in this life. You know, the ones that really helped make it all happen, whether it was words of encouragement, fixing random broken things (including my spirit), working to help make this dream a reality, or financial assistance.

CHAPTER 11: MESSAGE IN A BOTTLE

As we were gliding up to the dock, the dockmaster met us with a smile, "Good morning to you! That must've been a hell of a ride!" he called.

My co-captain and I shot glances at each other. *No kidding.*

After we were safely tied off, the client stumbled from his berth with his friend slowly dragging himself off the couch nearby.

"Fuel stop," my co-captain pronounced gaily, "We will be walking into town for a bite. We can meet back here in an hour."

The men were not looking too impressed, but we did not care. It would do us some good to have a little rest and some food. My co-captain took off in a random direction, so I decided to poke my head into a few of the little shops on my way to find food.

Wandering in through a lesser visited shop on a side street, my eyes filled with wonder. I had never seen such a beautiful display of handmade artistry using flotsam and jetsam found along beaches. One piece in particular caught my eye. Forgetting about my hunger, I placed the item on the counter and whiled away my shore time discussing the beauty of this life with the shop owner. I walked away with two gifts, one I purchased and one of joyful conversation.

"The hard work puts you where the good luck can find you." ("The Hard Work Puts You Where The Good Luck Can Find You.: Daily Success ...")

"Hello, is this Captain Jenn?" the man said as I answered the phone. After my reply, he continued, "My name is Walter and I would love to learn to scuba dive with your company, but I am unsure whether I would be mentally able to breathe through a regulator. Is there any chance I could try out one before I commit to classes?"

After several minutes of singing the virtues of scuba diving, and building his confidence, I decided to invite him down to the Yankee Sunshine. We were now in our third full season, and the summer rush had not started yet. It was Father's Day weekend on a Friday, and I did not have enough customers to make a sunset cruise happen. I had planned to don my scuba gear and jump in the river and clean the windows on the Yankee that evening anyway.

He was awaiting my arrival at the dock. Even the marina was quiet that evening. We were the only two around.

"Perfect," I said, after introducing myself. "I can show you how to gear up and give you a leg up for classes."

I let him try breathing air from my spare regulator, talked him through all the necessary steps I was taking to prepare to dive, invited him to step aboard the Yankee and watch me wash the windows from up above. During this process, Rob had shown up to gather the fuel tanks to refill for the next day's tours. The two climbed onboard to talk diving and watch.

I made a quick splash, and soon I was in another world. As a quick side note, if you have never been diving, you might not understand. As soon as I slip beneath the surface, everything changes. All the chaos in my mind is quiet. I must pay attention strictly to the tasks at hand or risk severe injury or even death. Suddenly, I am a part of another world, one that welcomes and is as curious to see me as I am to be there. There is an infinite number of things to explore, to understand. It always feels so much like *home* underneath the surface that it catches me off guard, no matter how many times I dive.

Gathering myself, I took the rag and finished the window washing quickly. Glancing upward, I could see the two of them talking, so I decided to spend some time underneath the surface to see if I could find a trinket that might keep Walter's interest peaked in scuba. As I swam around the bottom of the river, I picked up a few things, but was unimpressed with each item. I cannot describe it, but I wanted something *really special*, something unique.

Swimming toward the front of the boat, I noticed something green on the bottom, glistening in the remnants of the daylight. I swam over quickly and picked it up off the bottom. A unique little bottle! Turning it over in the palm of my hand, I could see there was something inside.

"A paper! Oh my gosh!" I thought. I quickly swam back to the boat, emerged from the water, and shouted for the spectators.

"Guys! Check this out! Rob, grab my phone please! We are going to want a picture of this!" the words tumbled out of my mouth excitedly.

The little green bottle was about 2/3 full of water and it was evident that there was a rolled-up piece of paper inside. Swiftly climbing aboard the Yankee Sunshine, the excitement was radiating off me. It was a scuba diver's dream come true! Hoping it was not a phone number rolled up inside, disconnected after 20 years, I began to tug at what was left of the cork. It was badly deteriorated. Rob took out his jackknife and scraped it away. The paper was wet and looked impossible to remove without damaging it.

"We'll just have to smash the bottle," said Rob, as anxious as I was to get at that note.

"No, let me go see if I can find something to finesse it out of there," I replied, not willing to smash the neat little bottle that had originally caught my eye.

Running into the marina building, my eyes scanning the workbenches for a tool that would fit the bill, they landed on a pick. *Perfect.* Not wanting the two guys to miss the big reveal, I scurried back out to the parking lot.

"I've got the perfect tool!" I shouted, running towards them.

The pick was like a tiny screwdriver with a half corkscrew at the end. I turned it in the paper and wiggled it out of the narrow neck of the bottle. As soon as it was an inch above the rim of the bottle, I set the tool down and grasped the paper, gently wiggling it free. Here was the moment of truth. I gently unrolled and unfolded the saturated paper. Rob had placed a piece of wood on the tailgate of his truck to set the paper on. As a curator at our local museum, he knew that the paper could be fragile.

We read the paper as a team, "Will the person who finds this paper, please return it to George Morrow, Cheboygan, Michigan. November 1926." Our eyes met. Unbelievable!

When I say I could not believe the luck, I mean it with every fiber of my being. For nearly two years the theme of my life was survival. Could it be that things were turning around? Either way, I was elated! I posted the find on my business Facebook page, fully expecting this to come full circle in about 45 minutes. Surely, we would have this bottle and the note back to 'Grandpa George' or his children soon. This was a small town find, after all. Clearly the bottle had gotten tangled up in weeds/current and traveled nowhere.

Clearly, Walter wanted to continue diving lessons. Rob insisted on taking the paper home with him and placing it in the freezer so that it would not disintegrate. Since the top was off my Jeep, I figured that was the safest place for it anyway. I put the little green bottle in the cup holder of my Jeep and took it home to share with the boys. All in a fun Friday evening on Father's Day weekend.

The next morning, I had some divers scheduled for a charter, so I was up and out the door before daylight. Gazing at the spectacular sunrise on our way offshore, I began to settle in to the cruise. You know how when something terrific happens the day before and you just come to realize it in the morning, adding it to your new reality? That was me, marveling in the wonder on the way out.

Once my divers were all safely underwater, I decided to check Facebook to see if we had any luck finding 'Grandpa George.'

Sitting on the deck of the boat, like a cat soaking up sunshine, I opened the app. To my utter amazement, my post had over 25k likes and comments. My inbox was exploding. Reading some of the comments had me laughing aloud.

"Uh, Rob, you're not going to believe this," I giggled, incredulously, reading some of the comments, "this guy 'Kevin' says this is definitely fake news. There is no way anyone would scuba in northern Michigan without a wetsuit. Here is a whole list of arguments for and against." I laid down on the deck and just laughed, belly laughed like I had not done in two years.

"I'm going to have to find this guy and thank him for the solid entertainment," I said, when I could finally breathe, wiping the tears from my face.

I had my first of many interview requests that morning, a news company out of Ohio. The sense of bewilderment was overwhelming. I did not know what to do with all of this.

The next day was Father's Day. I had gone downstate to visit my own Father, who was in an old folk's home. On my way back to Cheboygan to get on the boat for the day, I received a surprising phone call.

"Hi, Jennifer?" the lady on the phone said, "My name is Michele, and George Morrow was my dad. I still have his journal and the handwriting matches."

I could hardly believe my ears. It could not have been a more perfect day to be in touch with her.

My mom was riding in the car with me and took down Michele's information. I was anxious to meet her and give her the memento from her father. She mentioned she lives downstate and would like to come up after the busy summer season was over. Although I was anxious to meet her in person, I agreed it would probably be best. She was in her seventies and the roadways can get quite hectic with vacationers in the summer months.

Eventually, a myriad of news outlets caught on. We were in the New York Times, on CNN, on local news channels, doing radio interviews and podcasts, we even had a couple of interviews with news outlets out of Europe. The 'Guardian' sent a photographer to my home in Cheboygan! The summer was a whirlwind of interviews and business operations and keeping my teenage boys in check. 'Inside Edition' picked up the story and wanted to be in Cheboygan, filming when Michele came to meet me that fall.

'Hollywood' came, dressed just like you would expect, and it was all very exciting. What I did not expect was the *journal*. George Morrow served in WW2, and he wrote about the death of Hitler, the first man landing on the moon, and all kinds of events we only read about in history books. I took a picture of every page so that I could bask in it later when I had some time.

The miracles of the bottle infiltrate like tendrils of love. The notoriety for a newly formed business, the people I met as a result, the sheer joy it brought to my life is still very much an active part of my life. The miracles did not stop with me. Michele was reunited with a long-lost cousin, a best friend from her youth. I am asked to speak regularly on the miracle of the message in the bottle and use that story as inspiration and hope to those that may need it.

CHAPTER 12: FAITH

"**Where'd** you guys go?" Our client asked, bewildered.

My co-captain and I had met up again after I wandered out of the shop, just in time for him to steer me into the best restaurant in town to grab some takeout. We were carrying bags of food enough for us all.

"We got everyone some pizza and salads," I said, happy to be getting aboard the vessel again.

Climbing aboard, we quickly got underway. The client and his friend were in much better spirits now that the lake was calm and the fog had lifted.

Recognizing that he was a bit of a problem on the trip, the client sat down near to me. "Hey, I am sorry I was so nervous all along," he murmured, "I am not used to this at all, and I should have had some faith in you guys."

His apology was one any of us could murmur at any given time. We get stressed and anxious when we should have had faith all along.

Never be afraid to trust an unknown future to a known God. - Corrie Ten Boom

"Jenn, I have some terrible news," my aunt exclaimed with a wavering voice on the other end of the phone. This is the same aunt who, together with my mom, was extremely helpful with coming over on a whim to hang with the boys while I was working, showing support by making home cooked meals and hugs when I could not for the previous summer. "My daughter-in-law has a brain tumor, and she's seven months pregnant."

The news came during a time when I was bombarded with negative news of my own. I could not believe the bad luck. My gut instinct was to help in any way possible. The couple lives in Alabama and has a family of several more children to care for. My aunt was determined to make the trek down to help with the other kiddos.

"I will ask my mom if she can stay with the boys, and I will drive you down and hop on an airplane home," I said in a rush. It would only be three days, and I could not bear the thought of my aunt driving down alone in the inclement weather coming in. "Maybe I can bring some happiness to them too!"

My aunt and I had an uneventful drive down the country, talking and sharing advice with each other. We had always had a special bond, and it was a wonderful opportunity to express my gratitude for all she had done over the course of the last summer to help me out.

I had enough practice over the past year with positive affirmations and jumping hurdles and having FAITH that I had some viable advice for anyone headed into a storm.

Pulling into her driveway, their kids came rushing out to greet us. The air of stress washed over me like a wet blanket, heavy and familiar.

"Aunt Margie, would it be alright if I kidnapped Stacy and went down to the sea for one night?" I asked her on a whim, quickly getting the words out before she appeared outside with us. "Let's surprise her!"

"Ohhh, I love that idea! Yes, we will take care of the kids while you are gone!" she exclaimed happily.

After a delicious meal and some quick planning, we were off. Salt water heals everything, I was (still am) convinced, and I could have used some right then as well. We had an incredible heart to heart on the ride to the hotel, sharing stories of trauma and faith. We spoke of her doctor's appointments and why it is so important to believe the best outcome will be your outcome. After all, what good is it to stress yourself out? If there is one thing that I will always remember from my brother, it is that your life is a gift with an expiration date.

Pulling into the hotel, we began a tentative plan for the next day, our only day of vacation. We both agreed that the beach was where to find joy, even though the weather precluded us from swimming. I could not take away the stress for long, but I could help ease it for a moment. Sometimes, that is all it takes to remind someone who feels like they are drowning that their troubles are surmountable.

After picking up odd shells and playing on the beach for several hours, we decided to have a meal and head for home. She would drop me off at the airport hotel, and head back to her reality, I would hop on a plane in the morning and head for mine. I am not sure who benefitted more from the unexpected break, but it is safe to say we both needed it desperately.

Driving past a tattoo parlor, she exclaimed, "I am getting a tattoo! It will be this unalome, ending in the word 'faith.' It is ok if you do not want to, but I am!"

"The unalome symbol represents the path to enlightenment or to a higher place of spiritual contentment." ("Unalome Meaning in Yoga & Spirituality: Everything You Need to Know ...") It embodies our experiences as human beings on Earth and signifies a deeper awareness of how we move through life and learn from our actions. The unalome represents each person's life path. The path can be straight, circular, or winding, paved with anxiety, fear, joy, or love. The symbol is derived from Buddhism. To tie it with the word 'faith' made perfect sense to me.

I am definitely not one to make rash 'tattoo' decisions, but I found this one fitting. I would have the artist place it on my foot, so that when I look down in sadness or defeat, I can see this tattoo to remind me to have faith, that my life path is my own and I am paving the way.

"I'm in!" I exclaimed, "Let's do this."

It is always surprising to me when I learn life lessons. It was sometimes in school, sometimes at home, but most often they occurred when I was least expecting them. And usually I learned those lessons when I was taking the time to share some joy with others, in an effort that no one feels alone through painful experiences. This one three-day trip turned out to be exactly that. Putting each other's lives in perspective. Here was a woman with issues of her own, looking at a life-threatening issue to compound it, and she found faith through our conversations. We were able to lift each other's burdens, if only for a brief time.

Faith is a channel marker that, without it, I would have certainly given up. "Faith is the assurance of things hoped for, the conviction of things not seen." ("Hebrews 11:1 ESV - By Faith - Now faith is the assurance - Bible Gateway") It is trust, mine in God. So many people ask me where did I *find* this faith? No one likes the answer. Faith (at least for me) was not something I found just to grab up, easy as can be. I was desperate, at my absolute lowest. It was so *dark* that I had no choice but to keep moving forward in faith that things would have to get better. Only for so long (what seemed like an eternity), they kept getting *worse.*

Faith is believing that something better is just around the corner, even when the negatives keep piling up.

Faith is beginning to actively *look* for those things, knowing they might be small, but they are mighty. I can remember so many nights going to a secluded beach, after a long day of work, knowing the boys were asleep anyway and releasing the tears. Looking up at the water after those tears were done falling and thanking God that I had one private place to just regroup. One lit by the moonlight, dancing on the water.

Faith is writing a business plan with three children and believing it would work. It is making a plan to better your life, and the lives of those around you. It is throwing your hands up in the air and trusting (praying) that it will all come out for the better.

Faith is not knowing the details, but knowing the outcome will be what is meant for you.

Faith, for me, was knowing that I am made in God's image. I am important in this world. I have gifts to share. Faith is reading others' stories of darkness and feeling their triumph when they get to the other side. Faith, for me, is *believing*.

Faith is the middle name of my cousin's daughter, a sweet little girl that already made it through an insurmountable obstacle with her momma, even before birth. Faith is now so much a part of me that

people are incredulous at my apparently 'blind faith.'
I can promise you all, it is not blind. I have lived it.

CHAPTER 13: PERSEVERANCE (I'VE GOT THIS)

The whole group of us was in much better spirits after the food had been shared with lively conversation. We all ended with a better understanding of each other and our lives. As we were exiting the St. Clair River, we were gifted with the unbelievable luck of a 600' freighter in front of us.

"Oh, my goodness," the client breathed. Those were the only words spoken aloud as we passed the freighter on its starboard side. To see it pushing that volume of water within mere feet of our own vessel had us all awestruck. Even the music we were playing seemed to hush.

This life is so full of gifts. Sometimes they are hidden by heavy fog, but they are there. Passing the freighter in the dark had an entirely different feeling than passing one in the daylight, with calm seas and no fog. The gift during the dark was safety, the gift during the light was awe. Perseverance pays off.

Many of life's failures are people who did not realize how close they were to success when they gave up. - Thomas Edison

I awoke early, ready to fight the day. Ready to win this time. Yesterday's issues infiltrated my mind, but I shoved them off. Opening the fridge to grab a snack for breakfast before rushing off to the dive charter I was captaining that morning, I was greeted with a rush of *warm air.* "I just can't anymore," I thought to myself, in a rare moment of defeat.

Closing the fridge, I turned and walked calmly into my bedroom and ungracefully flopped down on my bed, face first. I had not cried at all. I was too busy being the strong one. The 'I got this' one. The refrigerator dying in the middle of summer (the summer from hell), when I simply could not afford to lose groceries, was the proverbial 'straw that broke the camel's back.' At that moment, the flood gates opened. I quietly sobbed and gave in to the feelings of defeat. I wallowed for as long as the clock would allow, before sopping up my face and heading out the door. *I can do this, keep going.*

On my way to the boat, the phone rang. It was my dad on the other end, "Hey Jenn, I'm just checking on you to see how things are going," he said, concern etching his voice.

Upon hearing his voice, the tears threatened again. Instead, I squared my shoulders and said, "My fridge is broken, I have no money to put food in it, let alone fix it," I said, self-pity making my voice waver.

"Don't you worry about a thing. I will contact your brother's friend and see if he can take a look. I am

108

paying for the repair. If he can't repair it, we'll figure out a different plan," he said with decisiveness.

A spark of hope began to enter my mind amidst the downtrodden attitude. "Pops, that fridge is older than me," I said, "but thank you for the hope."

"I got this," I thought with determination as I left the driveway, my self-pity in the rearview mirror.

I went to work, all three jobs that day, and at the very end of the day, relieved to be climbing in the front seat of the Jeep and headed home to my bed, I turned the key. Nothing. Not a whisper. It was after midnight, and I had long since forgotten about the fridge.

"Hey there, Jenn," an older gentleman walked up to my Jeep. He saw me with my head resting on the steering wheel and was concerned. We tried jump starting it, but there was nothing.

"It must be your starter. This is a manual transmission, we can pop the clutch and get ya home," he said.

"I've never done that before, can you teach me how," I asked, doubtful.

"Sure, it no big deal at all," he replied.

A quick tutorial and a pull, and it fired right up.

"Thank you so very much!" I exclaimed gratefully.

I did not have the time to feel relief, I was too busy paying attention to his directions and then wondering how I was going to get it started the next morning. I had to be at the dock at 7 am. Thinking things through, I decided to park on the back hill of my property and get myself to the marina the next morning by popping the clutch again. I'd worry about how to get home later.

"I've got this," I thought again. It was my mantra.

Later that night, when I arrived home, my fridge was working. It was humbling to think that some of my days were just being strung together by the kindness of others and my unfailing perseverance.

Perseverance is an interesting thing. How does someone know when they should persevere and when they should give up? During my marriage, I persevered until I genuinely thought it might kill me and my children. I wanted to leave several years before I did. The people that knew of the abuse were encouraging me to leave, just as I encouraged a battered coworker just two years earlier. Except she had bruises. All I carried was terror.

Instead, I thought about my vows, (through sickness and health and he was obviously sick). I thought about the scary statistics of issues for children of divorced families. I thought about how sad the loss of the family unit would be, (even though it was changing rapidly to dangerous). I thought about the disappointment of family members. I thought about the loss of extended family members. I worried about financial stability. I even thought about the Catholic church that we attended and how often I would pray for him to change or for me to change if I should. So, I persevered.

Looking back, now I can see that my perseverance was also self-preservation. If I did not have a viable plan, I would be just like any other statistic. According to a study published on apaservices.org, 50-68% of divorcing couples are victims of intimate partner violence. Sadly, I was never in the minority.

Perseverance looks similar in business. After failing at the grant opportunity, no perseverance would have had me scrapping the whole idea. Instead, (after the pity party in my head), I was looking for ways to make it happen still. I knew it would happen; I just did not know when. Then the phone call from the silent investor. My perseverance paid off this time.

Fast forward to now. We are going into our fifth season. At the completion of our last season, I was able to fully reimburse my silent investor with a card and a hefty check. In addition to that, I have created a fund to help women (and men, if the situation is similar).

In my letter to the Cheboygan Community Foundation:

> "I am honored to be able to pay him back this fall, but I would like to take it one step further. I would like to start a grant style program to be a guiding light out for other

111

women in abusive relationships with a plan for a better life, just needing the capital to start. While I could begin my own non-profit for this program, I am proposing that the Cheboygan Community Foundation use their 501-C3 status to collect the funds and distribute them (with my approval) to candidates that complete the application process. This will enable the Foundation to receive a higher level of visibility in our community, making this program a wonderful way to repay the generosity shown to me during that first exceedingly difficult winter."

Perseverance does not have a top tier. My mom's advice from so long ago still rings in my ears, "Just do your best, Jennifer."

That one piece of advice is my definition of perseverance.

CHAPTER 14: COURAGE

When we finally glided into Sinbad Marine and had the boat secure, we all breathed a sigh of relief. What a long journey we had, filled with trials of every kind. I was still delighted to have been a part of it and genuinely wished for another long ride back by boat.

"Thank you so much," the client gushed. He was greeted by many friends at the dock and was proud of his new purchase.

"Let me buy you both a beverage," his friend exclaimed.

"I'm in," I happily accepted. It had been a long journey, and I felt it would be a proper ending.

We all settled into the bar, happily recounting the trials and tribulations and beauty of our voyage. In the end, those trials made the beauty more of a marvel to us all.

Courage is the resistance to fear, mastery of fear, not absence of fear. -Mark Twain

"You are the most fearless person I have ever met," a close friend of mine confessed recently.

I sat there staring at him with my jaw dropped. Me? Fearless? And then I laughed, a genuine belly laugh.

After settling down a bit, I was still quite dumbfounded when I replied, "Is that what people see of me? That is pretty amazing and so not true!"

You might be thinking the same thing, after reading the story of me playing a game of 52 pick-up with my life. I can promise you, it is not that I am fearless; it is that I have developed courage. You see, one famous quote stuck with me over the years and has truly helped to shape my personality: It is not what happens to you; it is what you *do* with what happens to you.

Courage is a tricky one to pin down. It means such vastly different things to different people. What is easy breezy for one person may take the biggest act of courage for another. Courage is the ability to do something that frightens you. Alternatively, it can also be defined as strength in the face of pain or grief. One thing that courage is *not* is fearless. Little pieces of advice that have shaped my current definition of courage, and consequently, who I am, came over the course of my lifetime. I chose to pause in the moment, for whatever reason, and contemplate them as they came and allow them to help to define me. I am (of course) still learning today.

***

Several small instances of the practice of courage have shaped me, ones that felt monumental in the moment.

"Are you ready for that interview?" my best friend asked. I was about to interview for my first 'big girl' job as a teacher at 22, and I was nervous.

"Not at all," I confessed, "I am super nervous."

"Jennifer, take those nerves and pretend it is excitement," she advised.

I took that advice and let it sink in, "Could it be that easy?" I thought to myself.

For the rest of the day, I decided to just try it. It calmed my nerves, at least. I attended the interview and was hired for the job.

That weekend, I was waitressing at a local restaurant when a family came in for dinner before the young son's piano recital. The boy was in obvious distress, too nervous to even eat. After chatting with the family, I decided to share my bit of advice that I had been practicing.

"Can I help you try something new?" I asked the boy, making eye contact.

"Yes," he mumbled, clearly miserable with himself.

"Close your eyes, and just turn that nervousness into excitement," I said, eyes twinkling, "pretend it is excitement, that gets rid of the fear."

Now that advice I received helped another. Hopefully, it shaped that young man as well, and maybe even his own family now!

Fear comes in many different forms. That one piece of advice has helped me through some of the more minor fears of this life, but when it came time to face the fear of what I call playing 52 pick-up with my life, it was just a steppingstone to reach a whole new level. If you don't like what your life looks like, YOU have the power to change it within you. Imagine if you fail. So what, everyone does at some point. Now, imagine if you succeed. Every successful person has failed more often than they have succeeded. Get out there and burn through the failures so you can feel the success!

***

Everyday there is an opportunity to practice courage, faith, and perseverance. Do you have some social anxiety and want to change that about yourself? Get in your car and drive to the store. Challenge yourself to say hi to a complete stranger, with eye contact. (Courage) What is the worst that can happen? (Faith) Imagine the person is rude. Shrug your shoulders and try again. (Perseverance).

Do you feel 'stuck' in your life circumstances with no way out? Spend time thinking about a way out. Have faith, courage, and perseverance. Take the small steps. Dissect the issue into its small parts and work through them. It may seem like the most monumental mountain you or anyone has ever encountered, but you CAN climb it. Expect the stumbles, embrace the falls, surround yourself in the beauty of the life that was given to you.

On my bathroom mirror is a verse written in dry erase marker, "For the lord has not given us a spirit of fear, but of power, and love, and sound mind." It can also be found in the bible, 2 Timothy 1:7. This channel marker was guiding the way out of the storm of my life.

As for me, my ship is no longer in the tempest, I can slow my roll and help others see the lighthouse. I can continue to try and be a better human every day.

This is my story. It does not mean my life is all sunshine and rainbows. What this means is that I take time to pause and reflect often on my own character. If I notice something that I do not particularly like about myself, I do the work to change it.

What this means is that all I have learned over the course of my lifetime, but especially when I began to take the helm of my life back into my own hands, I can utilize when life becomes difficult. On the surface, I am a successful businesswoman, raising three teen boys, and 'living the dream.' The fact is all the heartache and lessons learned along the way brought me here. This is my own triumph, my ability to change this world for the better.

Come, take a ride with me aboard this beautiful vessel; the Yankee Sunshine, and experience the joy of this life!

Epilogue/Conclusion

I will never be done conquering the big waves. After all, it's good to stay in practice. Each winter, I tackle the other side of the business: marketing and numbers. It is all becoming less of a tsunami and more like a breezy day on the water. I will be content when it feels more like my favorite slow ocean roller.

My dreams are still supersize, and I am learning when to put a date and effort behind them. Sometimes it's best to let them come and pass. For now, I am raising those teenage boys and working hard every day at being the best mom I can be. In the wintertime, I'm remodeling my (now peaceful) home, learning new languages and traveling to places I have never seen. Oh, and this winter, I wrote a book. It takes incredible courage to move forward with big dreams. Publishing this book is no exception!

The rewards for living this life of courage, perseverance, and faith are limitless. I revel in them every single day. I invite you all to join me! I would be happy to teach you all I know about being the captain of your own ship. This journey starts with a dream.

A dream written down with a date becomes a goal. A goal broken down into steps becomes a plan. A plan backed by action becomes reality. (Quote by Greg Reid: "A dream written down with a date becomes a goal...")

Music You will Hear Aboard the Yankee Sunshine

Every song on the playlist is there for a reason. Many guests have requested the playlist, so here it is! Note, new songs are added regularly.

- A Pirate Looks at Forty (Jimmy Buffett)
- One Love (Bob Marley and the Wailers)
- Knee Deep (Zac Brown Band)
- Castaway (Zac Brown Band)
- Three Little Birds (Bob Marley and the Wailers)
- Island Song (Zac Brown Band)
- Buffalo Soldier (Bob Marley and the Wailers)
- It's a Beautiful Day (The Kiffness and Rushawn)
- Vacation (Dirty Heads)
- Soak Up the Sun (Sheryl Crow)
- Somethin' 'Bout a Boat (Jimmy Buffett)
- Listen to the Man (George Ezra)
- Hey Now Now (Michael Franti & Spearhead)
- The Great Lakes Song (Lee Murdock)
- I'm Not Running Anymore (John Mellencamp)

- All I Know So Far (Pink)
- Sunshine (Matisyahu)
- What a Wonderful World (Louis Armstrong)
- Steal My Sunshine (LEN)
- The Gambler (Kenny Rogers)
- Don't Stop Believing (Journey)
- Somewhere Over the Rainbow (Israel Kamakawiwo'ole)
- I Love My Life (Demarco)
- Something Just Like This (The Chainsmokers & Coldplay)
- Wildflowers (Live) (Jimmy Buffett)
- The Sound of Sunshine (Michael Franti & Spearhead)
- Thunder (Imagine Dragons)
- Riptide (Vance Joy)
- Life's Been Good (Dirty Heads)
- Rock Me Like the Ocean (Wheeland Brothers)
- Play That Song (Train)

Resources that helped along the way...

FOR THE DIVORCE

- One Mom's Battle | Divorcing A Narcissist with Tina Swithin (**www.onemomsbattle.com**)
  Mostly, I followed her on Facebook and educated myself on narcissistic abuse.

- DoctorRamani - YouTube
  BEST YouTube channel that helped me to understand what was happening. After I could see the patterns, I could conquer them!

- Divorcing a Narcissist: Advice from the Battlefield Paperback – February 20, 2014
  by Tina Swithin (Author) I kept this book under the carpet in my vehicle to read when I was alone.

- Several 'Surviving Narcissistic Abuse' pages on Facebook

- Don't forget your local Women's Resource Center, friends, and PRAYER.

FOR THE BUSINESS

- Think things through. Research EVERYTHING. Most of all, do what you love!
- Make your business plan. Be thorough. I used 'LIVEPLAN' to develop mine.
- Google business resources in your area. Our SBDC 'Small Business Development Center' was extremely helpful.

FOR MY LIFE

No judging, my music choice is eclectic and usually helps me get through the toughest parts of my life...here are some songs that helped along the way:

Goodbye Earl (Dixie Chicks)

Fight Song (Rachel Platten)

Glitter in the Air (Pink)

Better Life (Pink)

Beautiful Trauma (Pink)

Just Like a Pill (Pink)

Survivor (Destiny's Child)

Don't You Worry Child (Swedish House Mafia)

Broken Halos (Chris Stapleton)

The Gambler (Kenny Rogers)

Sorry Not Sorry (Demi Lovato)

Wagon Wheel (Darius Rucker)

Breathe In, Breathe Out (Jimmy Buffett)

No Woman, No Cry (Bob Marley)

Good Day (Greg Street Presents Nappy Roots)

I'm Not Running Anymore (John Mellencamp)

Whiskey in the Jar (Metallica)

Welcome (Metallica)

Seek and Destroy (Metallica)

Acknowledgments

Thank you to each and every one of you that helped along the way and that take the time to enjoy a ride aboard the Yankee Sunshine. My mom, for so many bits of wisdom, but especially for the key piece of advice: just do your best. My Dad, for always encouraging me to have fun and explore this life to the fullest. My boys, for being the absolute joy of my life. My Aunt for helping and praying our way through the tsunami. My editor Christine Nola for patience and cover design and keeping me off the ledge. For all of those who read the many revisions and offered their insight and made this the book it is.

This list could go on forever. This world is such a beautiful place, and the people in my circle are shining examples of that. For this fact, I am eternally grateful!

Did you enjoy Captain of My Own Ship? Please consider leaving an honest review on Amazon. It would help me a lot.

http://www.amazon.com/review/create-review?asin

About the Author

Jennifer Dowker is a Northern Michigan native. She is mom to three young men and several add on teens that find their way into her house and heart often. She is a successful entrepreneur and domestic violence survivor. She spends every minute she can on a boat or in the water and loves to meet new people and show them around her favorite place on Earth – the water.

Made in the USA
Monee, IL
11 July 2024